Christ on Trial

Christ on Trial

How the Gospel Unsettles
Our Judgement

Rowan Williams

William B. Eerdmans Publishing Company
Grand Rapids, Michigan / Cambridge, U.K.

ABC Publishing, Anglican Book Centre
Toronto, Canada

First published 2000 in Great Britain by HarperCollins*Religious*

This edition published jointly 2003 in North America by
Wm. B. Eerdmans Publishing Co.
255 Jefferson Ave. S.E., Grand Rapids, Michigan 49503 /
P.O. Box 163, Cambridge CB3 9PU U.K.
www.eerdmans.com
and by
ABC Publishing
Anglican Book Centre
600 Jarvis St., Toronto, Ontario, Canada M4Y 2J6
www.abcpublishing.com

Printed in the United States of America

07 06 05 04 03   7 6 5 4 3 2 1

Library of Congress Cataloging-in-Publication Data

Eerdmans ISBN 0-8028-2496-X

National Library of Canada Cataloguing in Publication

Williams, Rowan, 1950–
   Christ on trial : how the gospel unsettles our judgement / Rowan Williams.
ABC Publishing ISBN 1-55126-409-9
   1. Jesus Christ — Trial.   I. Title.
BT440.W44 2003   232.96′2   C2003-903853-X

Scripture quotations are taken from the Jerusalem Bible, © 1966 by Darton,
Longman and Todd Ltd and Doubleday

Contents

Introduction

The search for truth

We talk quite a lot about trials, in one way or another – not simply the kind that happen in courts of law, but 'trials' as a feature of ordinary life. We learn by trial and error; we give something a trial run. We talk of living in trying times, and say half-jokingly, 'These things are sent to try us.' We read of new drugs being given clinical trials; we hear of friendships being tried and true; people once spoke about trial marriages. What do all these usages have in common?

The simplest answer is that a trial is an attempt to find out the truth. We test a person, a medicine, a method of doing something, to discover what they really amount to, what they can 'deliver', to look beyond first impressions in order to understand more deeply how they work. It is this sense that is buried in our practice of calling proceedings in the law courts 'trials': someone is 'tried' in order to find out what they are really responsible for. The ambiguity in our use of the word is a fruitful one. Although we may talk about the trials of life in a way that suggests we are only thinking of irritating things we have to put up with, there remains an echo of the wider and more serious meaning of the word: if we do indeed have things we must put up with, this fact is bound up with the idea that our moral life is a process in which we shall find out truths about ourselves. The difficult, non-negotiable aspects of being human, in general and in particular, have the capacity to tell us things – often unwelcome things – about who or what we are.

God on trial?

Our religious tradition has much to say to us about this aspect – about trial as *discovery*. The Old Testament speaks more than once about suffering as a crucible in which the purity of a metal is tested, and its greatest and most disturbing meditation on what we might learn through the shapeless and arbitrary pain of the world is framed by scenes in a heavenly law court. Job does not know it, but he is 'on trial' in God's court so that it may be revealed how far his loyalty to God depends on the assurance that God will reward good behaviour. In this mythical framework, Satan is simply the prosecutor, the one whose job it is to raise doubts and to require evidence (though he is in fact allowed to act as an *agent provocateur*, goading Job into reaction).

What is remarkable in this strange book is that Job himself increasingly responds by demanding that *God* comes into court, that God should hear the case for the prosecution against himself. Some of the most anguished protests in the book express human frustration at the fact that God cannot be summoned to defend himself – or that, even if he could be so called to account, the disproportion between human complaint and divine power would make a fair trial impossible.

He whom I must sue is judge as well.
If he deigned to answer my citation,
could I be sure that he would listen to my voice?

(Job 9:15–16)

God, you must know, is my oppressor,
and his is the net that closes round me.
If I protest against such violence, there is no reply;
if I appeal against it, judgement is never given.

(Job 19:6–7)

How might God be brought to trial? How might he be brought to account? The answer given to Job, annihilating in its brutal simplicity, is that there can be no common language shared between creator and creature: there is only the possibility of amazement and silence. Other Old Testament texts go a little further. In Micah 6, for example, God brings Israel into court, but his plea reads more like a defence.

My people, what have I done to you,
how have I been a burden to you? Answer me.

(Micah 6:3)

God seems to be appealing against a decision by Israel, reminding them of his faithfulness. God, paradoxically, is the vulnerable one on this occasion, even though the prophet imagines God bringing the charges. If God's people will only look into their own history, they will see the truth. The trial of God will bring to light what God has shown himself to be across the centuries of Israel's history. And it is as if the lack of a common language means that it is God – not God's human partners – who is left silenced or struggling for words.

Test of character

All of this is in the background of the Gospel stories about
Jesus' trial, and some of the themes I have just sketched out
can, I believe, be identified in the way these stories are told,
along with a good many other issues. Another book could be
written on the whole language of 'temptation' in the Gospels
and, indeed, in later Christian thought: when we are told that
Jesus was 'tempted' in the desert, the word in Greek is the
same as for 'tried'. The temptations are a record of discovery,
and the way they are related makes it plain that their fundamental point is to do with who Jesus is.

It was Christianity that developed language about
temptation in the sense in which we now use the word – the
inclination to rebel against God, the law or goodness, understood as a test of integrity, an experience through which
something is brought to light about ourselves. Classical Greek
has no one word for what we mean by 'temptation', but,
prompted by the vocabulary of the Gospels and the theology
of experience as a probing of our truthfulness by God, the
Early Church refined the meaning of the straightforward
Greek vocabulary of testing until it came to refer fundamen-
tally to the inner struggles of the moral and spiritual self.
Peirasmos and similar words in Greek had once meant testing
in the widest sense. By the fifth Christian century, they
referred primarily to aspects of the soul's dialogue with itself.
'Temptations' could be catalogued and analysed and various
strategies defined for avoiding them.

So obvious did this seem, that the petition in the Lord's
Prayer, 'lead us not into temptation', came to be understood
universally as a plea not to be too easily seduced by wicked

inclinations – while its original sense was undoubtedly a plea to be spared the coming test represented by the end of the age. The sufferings that would wind up the existing order would prove a crucible for the testing of hearts, and believers in the earliest generations prayed that their present allegiance to Jesus would be made strong enough for them not to experience the end times as this sort of painful probing.

The chapters that follow attempt to trace the ways in which the evangelists let the truth of and about Jesus emerge in the way they narrate his trial. Since, as the Old Testament begins to suggest, it is also *we* who are on trial when we attempt to bring God to judgement, these reflections also touch on what it is about us that comes to light when we are faced with Jesus as he stands before his judges. Furthermore, because this double-directional trial, God's and ours, is not simply a matter of historical record but is enacted in every encounter of faith, I have added some thoughts on the trials of Christ's followers, the martyrs, and on some modern re-creations of the character and fate of Jesus' judges.

Historical details

What I have not attempted to do is to offer any sustained discussion of the historical and critical problems around the trial stories. A formidable scholarly literature has built up on this subject, especially in the last 30 years, but no very clear consensus has been reached. Conclusions vary from a confidence that the evangelists were fully and accurately informed of the procedures of Jewish and Roman courts to a radical scepticism about every single detail of the Gospel accounts. The matter has been a good deal complicated by the question of whether the desire to play down Roman involvement in the condemnation of Jesus led the evangelists to give more weight than they should have done (strictly historically) to the role of the Jewish authorities; and by the related question of whether, if Jesus was really executed for sedition against the Roman government, there has been a considerable smoothing over of the political elements in his ministry.

My own view, for what it is worth, is that Mark, Matthew and Luke are not likely to have known all that much about the processes of the Jewish courts and consequently assume that Jesus received from the Jewish authorities a more formal condemnation than was probably the case. John, who does frequently show signs of first-hand knowledge of matters in Jerusalem, is far more likely to be right in describing a hurried and irregular hearing in the High Priest's residence, designed to establish charges. However, the references in the other Gospels to a charge of threatening to destroy the Temple may well reflect a persistent tradition that this was something raised as a possible charge in the high-priestly circle.

No one today is in a position to know what, if anything, in John's extraordinary dialogue between Jesus and Pilate is actually reportage. Here, more than almost anywhere else, a concern about whether this is exact history can distract us from the central issue, which is our dialogue with Jesus through the medium of the inspired narrative. As for the nature of the charges and their political content, we must assume that, whatever was said about blasphemy in the hearings before the priests, the substantive charge must have been related to threats of civil disorder, simply because crucifixion was legally the punishment in such cases – and the charges relating to the Temple are likely to have been decisive here, as a good many modern scholars, both conservative and liberal, have argued.

Drama and challenge

The evangelists are recording a series of events marked by violence and confusion. Even on the most conservative estimate of their accounts, there must have been episodes imperfectly seen or understood, episodes where direct eyewitness evidence was lacking, along with partially conflicting testimonies. To grant this is simply to allow that the inspiration of the Gospel narratives is not the gift to the writers of a miraculous God's-eye view. If Jesus' life is a truly human one, the witness to his life must be human as well, and human witness is seldom straightforward or comprehensive. If the historical trial of Jesus was a rapid blur of events – an arrest at midnight, a hasty series of incomprehensible legal or semi-legal procedures, followed by public humiliation and torture – it should not surprise us that the records are less than calm and dispassionate, that they read like fragments pieced together in the aftermath of a traumatic disaster.

This also means that they are not best read as either good or bad transcripts of proceedings that are taking place or have taken place somewhere else. The evangelists use the very confusion and tumult of the story as an opportunity to involve the reader in the drama. The variations in detail and emphasis between the Gospel accounts represent different ways of involving us, different ways of exposing us to discovery and self-discovery. Faced with the Jesus of these narratives, we are needled and prompted into the kind of response that will tell us what we never recognized about ourselves before, as well as what we never knew about God. The Gospels overall are a contemporary challenge more than a bare historical record, and this is seldom more true than in the stories of the trial and the passion. Some modern scholars have argued that the passion stories began as a series of 'readings' to be used by believers tracing the last hours of Jesus through the streets of Jerusalem, a sort of primitive 'Stations of the Cross'. It is certainly true that they have always had the character of liturgy and drama; they have always required the reader to *stand* in particular places, to find himself or herself somewhere in the map traced by the history of Jesus in his suffering, and so to find truth and judgement.

This book is an invitation to read the familiar stories with all this in mind: to be judged, but also to be released by that judgement into the light of truth, and to find in the prisoner at the bar the final clue to what we are and what we may be in God's sight; to find in him also the final clue to the nature of our maker and redeemer and some pointers to where he may be recognized now.

CHAPTER ONE

Mark: Voices at Midnight

Vivid drama

The way Mark tells his story has a quality more like film than anything else. Some kinds of narrative obviously expect you to take time reflecting, making connections, looking back to check and compare, but this is a story which moves you on relentlessly, breathlessly. Of course you can spend time – a lifetime – reflecting, analysing, making connections. People have done just that, for centuries. But the first impression refuses to go away: this is a text full of urgency. Anyone who has ever done any study of the New Testament knows that just about the commonest Greek word in Mark's Gospel is *euthus*, 'straight away'. Episode follows episode with a tumbling rapidity. If you try to calculate the length of time Jesus' ministry must have taken on the basis of Mark's narrative, you would come up with a guess of a few weeks at most.

When Pasolini made his great film *The Gospel According to St Matthew* in the 1960s, he showed a Jesus consumed with this same kind of urgency, striding ahead of the disciples, throwing strange words over his shoulder. It is there in Matthew, certainly, but the feel of Pasolini's presentation is much more like Mark. Mark's Jesus does not normally stop to explain anything, or give any continuous teaching. Nothing is said about his origins or early years. He steps out suddenly against a dark background. Sometimes he seems to lash out in protest against the foolishness of those nearest him. In Chapter 8, for example, after the miracle of the feeding of the 4,000, the Pharisees ask for a sign and he responds 'with a sigh that came straight from the heart' (v. 12). But then, as he talks with his disciples in the boat and they fail to grasp the meaning of the miracle, Jesus berates them fiercely: 'Do you not yet understand? Have you no perception? Are your minds closed?' (v. 17).

Worse follows: Peter's profession of faith leads into the awful anticlimax of his protest about Jesus' coming suffering, and Jesus rounds on him: 'The way you think is not God's way but man's' (v. 33). So it goes on. Jesus knows more than he can say; he is like a naturally gifted musician trying to explain to slow or even tone-deaf listeners how basic harmony works. And when the transforming power of his presence breaks through in healing, he hurries to forbid people to talk about it. It is as if he knows they will only find the wrong words, the wrong categories. So he presses on, *euthus*, without delay, to the goal that no one around him wants to think about or understand.

As the last act of the drama begins in Chapter 14, the pace of the storytelling slows down in one way. From now on, each episode is presented with far more detail; we are escorted from place to place in Jerusalem in the course of one night – a night that takes as long to describe as much of the weeks, months or years that have led up to it. In another way, however, the technique of the story is the same, and the hurried images flash past as they do in a film. Even more than in earlier chapters, you have a sense of intense, rapid, *physical* movement. There is violence around, the camera is jostled, a bright light shines in your face, then there is a blur of confused activity. All around you can hear or half-hear voices, but you cannot quite make out what they are saying.

A senseless nightmare

Still more marked, though, is the sense of bewildering *absurdity* in it all. The sentence is settled in advance; the problem is finding evidence. As Lewis Carroll wrote in *Alice's Adventures in Wonderland*: "'Let the jury consider their verdict,'" the King said, for about the twentieth time that day. "No, no!" said the Queen. "Sentence first – verdict afterwards."'[1] Mark's trial scenes are more like those in *Alice* than any more conventional legal process. Or, to pick up a more serious echo, they are like Kafka's terrible and prophetic fantasies in *The Trial*. The process does not make sense – perhaps it is not meant to. Kafka's hero, Joseph K., is arrested without knowing what the charge is; he is unable to discover what he is accused of, despite increasingly desperate efforts; he infringes unknown procedural rules; his protests turn against him; at last, pathetically and apparently arbitrarily, he is knifed in a disused quarry. The real terror of this story is the growing certainty that no sense can be made of what is happening. As Kafka himself said, it is as if we know we are guilty, but not what we are guilty of. We are going to die, but we are denied the satisfaction of knowing why.

1 Lewis Carroll, *Alice's Adventures in Wonderland*, London: HarperCollins, Armada edition, 1990, Chapter 12, p. 136.

This is where Mark's trial scenes speak most eloquently to our own century, to the contemporary horrors of the dissolution of law. Think of the show trials that took place in 1930s Moscow; the racist murderers acquitted in the American South a generation ago (even now, you can hardly say that issue has gone away, either in the USA or nearer to home; the case of Stephen Lawrence is a prime example); the national leaders put on trial by the new military regime. This is the world of the door broken in at five in the morning, the interrogation block, the questions you cannot understand, to which you cannot guess the right answers, the hustling from place to place in sealed vans, the wrapped bundle dropped by the side of a country road. Calm and stony, the authorities state their case. He was guilty of extensive tax offences. He was in a disturbed state at the time of arrest. No, we cannot guarantee to supervise prisoners all the time. Yes, it appears that he committed suicide. We deeply regret her death. It would be outrageous to make political capital of this by suggesting that government employees were in any way involved. No appeal will be considered; interference by foreign governments would be most unwelcome. Sentence was passed seven years ago; administrative complications have delayed the execution; it is irrelevant that he has been described as mentally retarded; his race is immaterial to the decision.

When you are caught up in such a world, power appears to be purely and simply unaccountable, in both senses of the word. It is answerable to no one, and you cannot give a rational account of how it works. Of course, this is not by any means an exclusively twentieth-century problem. Readers of Umberto Eco's *The Name of the Rose* will recall the proceedings of the Inquisition described in the book, an episode that is in fact drawn almost word for word from a fourteenth-century manual for judges in the Inquisition's courts, which gives careful advice on how to interpret apparently innocent replies in a heretical sense. Nonetheless, it is our own age that has virtually normalized these nightmares in so many states and has hugely increased the resources that can be used for surveillance, just as it is our own age that has made such practices alarmingly common for some categories of supposed offenders, even in countries with healthy legal traditions. If the scenes sketched above appear to belong in distant countries with barbarous governments, reflect for a moment on the experience of those charged with illegally entering Britain in recent years.

Jesus breaks his silence

Mark's narrative resonates with this midnight world. He takes us into a place where we can only hear unfamiliar and menacing voices in the dark. We are not meant to understand how the world goes. Jesus is arrested, hustled in the dark to a private and illegal hearing where corrupt witnesses have been procured to provide material for the charge sheet. The story that emerges is insufficiently consistent, however, and the High Priest eventually invites the prisoner to incriminate himself. 'Are you the Christ,' he asks, 'the Son of the Blessed One?' (14:61). And Jesus breaks his silence – not only the silence he has kept during the trial so far, but also, more significantly, the silence of the whole Gospel. All the way through he has held back, has forbidden any mention to be made of his status as God's Son. He has silenced the demoniacs, the healed leper, Simon Peter, but now he breaks open these carefully

constructed secrecies with the plainest of plain words: 'I am'
(v. 62). Why?

Throughout the Gospel, Jesus holds back from revealing
who he is because, it seems, he cannot believe that there are
words that will tell the truth about him in the mouths of others. What will be said of him is bound to be untrue – that he
is master of all circumstances; that he can heal where he wills;
that he is the expected triumphant deliverer, the Anointed. In
Anita Mason's novel *The Illusionist*, this is hauntingly
expressed in the reworking of the scene of Peter's confession,
where Jesus, in response to what Peter says, replies, 'You have
said something that should never have been said, and there
will be a heavy price to pay . . . There is a kind of truth which,
when it is said, becomes untrue.'[2]

Remember, the world Mark depicts is not a reasonable one;
it is full of demons and suffering and abused power. How, in
such a world, *could* there be a language in which it could truly
be said who Jesus is? Whatever is said will take on the colouring of the world's insanity; it will be another bid for the
world's power, another identification with the unaccountable
tyrannies that decide how things shall be. Jesus, described in
the words of this world, would be a competitor for space in it,
part of its untruth.

The time for truth

This is where the meaning of the trial becomes clear, where we
see what truth it is that this trial establishes. Jesus before the
High Priest has no leverage in the world; he is denuded of

2 Anita Mason, *The Illusionist*, London: Abacus, 1983, p. 127.

whatever power he might have had. Stripped and bound before the court, he has no stake in how the world organizes itself. He is definitively outside the system of the world's power and the language of power. He is going to die, because that is what the world has decided. It is at this moment and this moment only that he speaks plainly about who he is. He names himself with the name of the God of Israel, 'I am', and tells the court that they will see the Human One seated at God's right hand, coming in judgement. Humanity does not live in this world of insane authorities, but with God. When God's judgement arrives, it will be in the unveiling of a true human face as opposed to the masks and caricatures of the High Priest's world.

Mark is inviting us to think again about what we mean by transcendence. Normally, when we use such words, we think of God's surpassing greatness, but how can we avoid that becoming simply a massive projection of what *we* mean by greatness? If that is the case, we shall, like Peter in the Gospel story, rebel against what God actually desires to do and to be in the life and death of Jesus. If we are really to have our language about the transcendence – the sheer, unimaginable *differentness* – of God recreated, it must be by the emptying out of all we thought we knew about it, the emptying out of practically all we normally mean by greatness. No more about the lofty distance of God, the sovereignty that involves control over all circumstances: God's 'I am' can only be heard for what it really is when it has no trace of human power left to it; when it appears as something utterly different from human authority, even human liberty; when it is spoken by a captive under sentence of death.

The freedom or power at issue here, in such an utterance at such a time, is the freedom of complete alienation from the categories of the unaccountable world, freedom from the insanity and violence of human power. I said that Mark's passion story gave the impression of voices in the dark. You could say more: that God's voice here is supremely a voice at midnight, audible only when the language of this world has fallen away once and for all around the figure of the prisoner on trial. There is nothing comforting, edifying or reassuring, nothing that secures our picture of ourselves and our hopes for ourselves, in the silent prisoner. And that is how and why we can hear him name himself with God's name.

Jesus breaks his silence at this moment in the trial because only now can what he says be heard. There is little or no danger that we shall now mistake what he means, that we shall confidently describe him in words that reflect our own aspirations. He is who he is, and we can do nothing but let our imagination and our language be reshaped by him – if, that is, we have ears to hear, if we are not already determined to abide by the standards of the insane world that has brought him to trial. Nothing is left to him now: from this point on in the passion story, the only words he speaks are in the despairing cry from the cross, 'My God, my God, why have you deserted me?' (15:34). He has nothing to say to Pilate (in stark contrast to the Jesus of John's Gospel, with his oracular challenges to the governor), and he has nothing to *do* except die. Once he has spoken to the High Priest, he is immediately handed over to the mob to be abused and beaten up. Invited to 'play the prophet', he says nothing. His prophetic word, like his transforming action, is now only in his suffering and dying.

Either we see that the whole story of Mark's Gospel leads here, to this restored silence, or we abandon the attempt to make any sense of it. Jesus has held back from declaring who he is all through the Gospel because up until the trial he was still able to do and say things, to be someone acting alongside others in the world. Up to this point it was still possible to misunderstand him as a great man, a wonderworker, someone who might compete successfully with other sorts of power in the world. But not now.

In this sense, Mark's trial narrative passes sentence on our understanding of power and significance. Without this strange moment at the heart of the trial, we might be left with a false clarity about God and how God is recognized in Jesus: God becomes the illustration of what is highest or strongest for us. This applies not only to the crude identification of God with success or domination, and the resulting belief that failure in the world's terms somehow indicates God's absence; it applies also to the identification of God with what seems to us wisest or holiest, most spiritually impressive. But here, the one who says 'I am' is, at that moment, in that setting, neither wise nor holy, neither admirable nor impressive. He has 'no looks to attract our eyes' (Isaiah 53:2). If we are prepared to listen for a moment to the extraordinary idea that this is indeed the very self of God standing before the court, it is we who are silenced, we who have our careful and exact expectations overturned.

'Here I stand'

This in turn puts to us the question of where we now expect to see or hear God most clearly. Against the court's insanity, Jesus simply is who he is; he does not seek to justify this in terms of success, and he is not the person he is because of the results assured. It may be that, in the light of Mark, we see and

hear God most clearly in such moments of obstinate detachment from results and successes. People at times make ges-
tures and take stands, not for the sake of dramatizing their
beliefs or for the sake of any result that might be guaranteed,
but because there is simply nothing else that can be done with
honesty. Turn back in the Bible to the book of Daniel, and you
will find just this in the story of the three young men condemned to death by King Nebuchadnezzar.

> **Shadrach, Meshach and Abednego replied to King**
> **Nebuchadnezzar, 'Your question hardly requires an**
> **answer: if our God, the one we serve, is able to save us**
> **from the burning fiery furnace and from your power,**
> **O king, he will save us; and even if he does not, then**
> **you must know, O king, that we will not serve your**
> **god or worship the statue you have erected.'**
>
> (Daniel 3:16–18)

'Even if he does not' – the act does not depend on the outcome, it is simply what has to be done. The author of Daniel
would have had in mind all those in his own day who had
resisted the persecution of King Antiochus and who had not
been rescued, as the three young men in the story were. He is
recording the bare fact that those who resisted did so knowing
that miraculous rescues were not in the contract.

What is the use of resistance like this? Iris Murdoch's novel
An Accidental Man turns largely on the struggle of a young
American, Ludwig Leferrier, to decide whether he should
return to the USA to face possible imprisonment for refusing
the Vietnam draft, or whether he should settle down to an
academic life in Britain with a delightful young heiress. What

is the *point* of going home? It will not affect the outcome of the war; the only sure result will be the ruining of his personal and professional life. He searches desperately for wisdom. At first, he looks for someone to absolve him, to tell him that it is indeed all right not to return. Later, however, facing the realities of death and failure around him and feeling that his own moral being is slipping away, he breaks his engagement and goes back – only to be rapidly forgotten by the other characters in the novel, even, it seems, by his former fiancée. As he discusses the decision he faces with an older man with a reputation for some sort of spiritual insight, he hears from him a story from Eastern Europe about protest under a totalitarian regime:

> They were holding a board protesting against the trial of a writer . . . They looked so lonely and sort of gratuitous and aslant, if you know what I mean, like something in a corner of a painting. And of course everyone who passed by looked the other way and quickened their step as soon as they saw what was going on. Then I saw a man coming along who looked as if he too would pass by. He hesitated and he looked round, and then he came back and began shaking hands with them. That shaking hands – I can't describe it – it was suddenly as if that place had become the centre of the world.[3]

'The centre of the world' – this is a kind of statement not unlike the 'I am' of Jesus' trial. Later in the novel Ludwig, who

3 Iris Murdoch, *An Accidental Man*, London: Penguin, 1971, p. 273.

has made up his mind to return home and face prosecution and imprisonment, is talking to the same man, trying to make the link between the huge, abstract issues and his own chance circumstances. The link, he says, is where God would live 'if God existed'; but even if there is no God, the link is real:

> 'So there is a link?'
> 'There are two pure things juxtaposed.'
> 'Simply juxtaposed?'
> 'Simply pure.'[4]

This is an attempt to identify the point where God 'comes in', where God becomes manifest. Even the nonbelieving characters of the novel recognize that there is something appallingly mysterious about the sense of obligation, even compulsion, that can make someone take a choice that can have no apparent effective outcome, that will put everything at risk without necessarily making any difference to the world's injustices.

So it is that Mark's Jesus at his trial becomes a revelation of where God is: God is simply that which makes it natural and necessary to act against insanity and violence. God is the reality that, simply by being what it is (or who it is), establishes that violence cannot fill up the whole space of the world. *At this moment*, God is not and cannot be what guarantees success or provides a convincing explanation of the strange behaviour of those who refuse the world's ways. That would be to let God become again a competitor in the world's business, whose power can 'trump' all other claims at the end of the day. In making these decisions, in taking up these

4 Ibid., p. 434.

positions under judgement, there can be no simple assurance of final victory.

Jesus in Mark's account tells the court that they will see the Human Form seated at God's right hand, coming on the clouds. Yet this is not the prophecy of an escape or a revenge. In its context, it is more obviously the reinforcement of what has just been said in Jesus' statement, 'I am.' The Son of the Blessed One is indeed the silent prisoner; the condemned human form is what God will show as he comes in glory. The reality or – could we say? – the 'worthwhileness' of God is not in the promise of safety, the possibility of escape from the world; there is only the recognition here and now of God's glory in the freedom that appears when the insane violence of the world meets immovable resistance.

'God for nothing'

In H.F.M. Prescott's panoramic fiction about the English Reformation, *The Man on a Donkey*, events move towards a nightmare conclusion – betrayal, despair, sheer pain of mind and body – as the northern rebellion of Robert Aske dissolves in humiliating failure and the specific human consequences work themselves out. The sharp, worldly Prioress of Marrick, Christabel Cowper, finds herself defeated in her passionate struggle to save her convent, and is confronted by an elderly nun at the house she is staying at in London, who tries to explain to her that the coming disaster may be a sign of God's judgement, so that the monks and nuns may rediscover who he truly is. Christabel protests:

> The Prioress of Marrick stared to hear this gentle
> creature turn upon her. She was even a little
> impressed; not very much, but enough to make her
> argue the point.
>
> 'But though He bless,' she said, 'what then?'
>
> 'What then?'
>
> 'If we – if you shall have lost all, and are turned
> out and the House fall. . ? Then it will be too late.'
>
> 'Too late for what?'
>
> The Prioress of Marrick, thinking in terms of a
> bargain between buyer and seller, found herself
> unwilling to use the first words that came to her
> tongue, 'Too late for payment.'[5]

Christabel cannot hear what the old sister's midnight voice
is saying: that the religious life is no bargain, no economic
contract assuring reward; that the threat and terror of the
Dissolution is somehow built into the practice of the life itself.
Worse is to come. Aske, the leader of the rebellion, has been
betrayed by his friends, the king has ignored promises of safe
conduct, and he is hanged in chains at York. Dying in extreme
agony of mind and body, these are his thoughts:

> God did not now, nor would in any furthest future,
> prevail. Once He had come, and died. If He came
> again, again He would die, and again, and so for ever,
> by His own will rendered powerless against the free
> and evil wills of men . . . But yet, though God was not
> God, as the head of the dumb worm turns, so his

5 H.F.M. Prescott, *The Man on a Donkey*, London: Penguin, 1952, 1969, p. 707.

> spirit turned, blindly, gropingly, hopelessly loyal,
> towards that good, that holy, that merciful, which
> though not God, though vanquished, was still the last
> dear love of a vanquished and tortured man.[6]

'God for nothing' – it was the title of a book some years ago
that sought to challenge some of the ways in which we domes-
ticate our language about God. To speak of God as being seen
most clearly in situations where the service of God offers no
possible success, where even the hope of eternal life is so
abstract that it might be a proposition in higher mathematics,
is often to invite protest. This cannot be *gospel*, surely? It does
not sound like good news. But the challenge remains, to
re-imagine what it is for God to speak to us *as* God – not as a
version of whatever makes us feel secure and appears more
attractive than other familiar kinds of security. For if our talk
about God is a religious version of talk about human safety,
the paradox is that it will fail to say anything at all about
salvation. It will not have anything to do with what is deci-
sively and absolutely *not* the way of this world.

Religious speculation talks a good deal about transcendence. What Mark's Gospel suggests, throughout the narrative
but above all in the trial story, is that we cannot properly think
of transcendence merely by projecting what we know and
what seems to help and reassure us to the highest point
imaginable. Transcendence meets us, and surprises us, when
we are shown simply that the way of this world is not the final
and exclusive truth. What Robert Aske blindly senses as good,
holy and merciful just is what it is, for its own sake; it has its

6 Ibid., p. 765.

substance in itself, not in its dependence on any outcome. It is not a strategy for attaining something other than itself; it needs nothing else. When the vanquished and tortured man in the Gospel story says, 'I am,' to his tormentors, he claims exactly that character of independence – he is something that is for its own sake and needs no justification.

The ongoing story

Of course, it is not the case that Mark denies that the life of Jesus makes all the difference to the way the world goes – his Jesus is pre-eminently healer, exorcist and wonderworker. Nor does he end his Gospel at Calvary. Yet by underlining Jesus' reluctance to be pigeonholed as healer, exorcist and miracle-man, by underlining the 'messianic secret', he says, in effect: if Jesus truly makes *all* the difference, beware of reducing this difference to a series of spectacular improvements in the human condition. Whatever he makes possible must be more than this.

It is the same with the resurrection. Mark is at his most enigmatic here, leaving us with the silent terror of the women at the tomb, not with a triumphant vindication. Once again, he invites us to consider what difference the resurrection makes. Is it a reversal of tragedy? A happy ending? A promise of revenge against the sinful judges who brought Jesus to his death? It is none of these. The resurrection comes across as radically unexpected, almost disconnected with what has gone before. It is as if the resurrection is like the moment of revelation at the trial: it is what it is; it is the bare fact that the life of Jesus is not contained or swallowed up by the way of this world, not even by the 'natural' ways of death and corruption.

The freedom revealed at the trial becomes materially visible in the empty tomb – yet, as Mark's Gospel ends, we are told nothing of what this might mean in any concrete sense. As has sometimes been said, the *reader* is the 'lost ending' of Mark. We have to discover for ourselves what difference is made by this life, this death and this disorienting mystery after the crucifixion.

The Gospel, in other words, is kept alive in its telling and communication by reminders of how strange its central claim is – that God has acted to remake the world from within, from within a life that is ended by desertion and failure and appalling suffering. Since it truly is *God's* action that is involved, the death that appears to end the story fails to do so – which is why the story is presented to us now for our conversion and transfiguration. We learn to read Mark's Gospel best when, as a community of people reading in faith, we are aware of lives and narratives that repeatedly re-present this aspect of the Gospel; when we are able to reflect on stories and styles of life in the community that show something of the 'obstinate uselessness' of witness to God's truth.

Later in this book, we shall be looking at how the stories of the martyrs functioned, especially in the Early Church, as points of reference for some sense of Christian integrity – and at some of the ways in which even these stories can be domesticated in turn. We have already noted in passing how the vowed life of monks or nuns can work in the same way, as testimony to the 'for its own sake' character of following Jesus. Here too the history of the Church shows clearly enough that Christabel Cowper's approach has remained popular, and that what began as a costly witness can become an immense transaction in spiritual economics – so much renunciation for a higher reward.

Accepting the present

One more thing is worth noticing about this. Our attitude to *time* is challenged and judged. It is quite possible to persuade people of the importance of present renunciation, in the face of present apparent failure, when there is a sure promise of how things will turn out for the best in the future. We are encouraged to make the present that bit less real than the future, and within this is a rather problematic element. We are being told that the present is somehow less real than the future, even though we know perfectly well that the future is not actually *there* in the way the present moment is. This can be the beginning of an attitude that is always trying to escape from the present – or worse, trying to deny the harshness of someone else's present because of the future that *I* believe in. Again, this is all too recognizable a problem in religious history. It can be one of the most insidious ways in which religious power is corruptly exercised: telling people that their actual present experience is what they must ignore if they wish to be faithful believers.

The hard thing to accept about the faith of Mark's Gospel, or of the three young Jews in the book of Daniel, or of Robert Aske hanging in his chains, is that there is no simple denial of the terrible character of the present moment, no way of escaping into the future. The idea of a future hope is not, of course, absent in the Gospel. Jesus' response to the High Priest speaks of the coming in judgement and glory of the 'Human One' who will put God's will into effect on this earth. The judges of the earthly court will see this coming. Yet here is the strange thing: Mark is writing for people who know perfectly well that the judges of that court did *not* see any coming in glory. They are either dead or, like Mark's readers, living in the indeterminate period between resurrection and judgement. What the priestly judges *have* seen is the crucifixion and the faith of the community. This is all there is for what you might call public consumption, because the resurrection in Mark's story is so evidently a matter of silent, terrifying knowledge that cannot really be communicated in simple words. So the response of Jesus at the trial cannot be translated as if it were saying, 'Soon you'll see that I was right, soon the tables will be turned.' Somehow the coming of the Human One in judgement is inseparable from the historical moment of Jesus' death and the present struggles of the community to keep faith.

So Mark tells his Church that the last thing they should be doing is turning their eyes away from the two things that other human beings see – the cross and the reality of their life together. The cross is scandal enough, you might think, but Mark notoriously presses on the raw nerve of the stupidity and unfaithfulness of Jesus' disciples. What is the 'present moment' of the Church's life like? Well, it is all too like the response of the disciples in Jesus' lifetime. How very tempting, then, to turn our emotional energy and imagination towards a 'better' Church, away from the embarrassing present moment. Nonetheless, it is here, in Jesus crucified and in the struggling and failing community, that the coming of the Human One in glory is made visible to the world.

It is a vision that the contemporary Church might well ponder. Paraphrasing St Paul, we might say that 'liberal' Christians look for a clear and purified future and 'traditionalists' look towards a more faithful and less compromised past. Yet the gospel remains the gospel of the crucified, asking of us an attention to the reality that is before us and within us here and now, a reality that will be scandalous and painful. Pascal's stark assertion that 'Jesus will be in agony until the end of the world' is much in the spirit of Mark; and it is not an observation about the deplorable state of unbelievers, but an exhortation to believers to keep awake – awake to their own inability to stay in the almost unbearable present moment where Jesus is – rather than look for an unreal future or past to run to.

Perhaps the hardest thing of all for the Christian is precisely this bearing with the present moment, not pretending that it is necessarily good or happy, but simply acknowledging that it is here, 'on this lowly ground', in John Donne's words, that God is to be met, whether for joy or for terror. Something of this comes through in the language of the Eastern Church about the Eucharist. The *now* of the eucharistic celebration is a state of being contemporary with Christ in his past and his future – the cross, the empty tomb and the coming again are all here and now as we make our common thanksgiving.[7] The mystery is in our midst, wherever and however we find ourselves.

The still point of the world

That is why, in a surprising way, the Gospel of Mark, apparently so full of rapid movement and disorientation, is also a call to a particular kind of contemplation and stillness. Learning to pray requires, as the books will tell you, a willingness to 'put

7 I have in mind the prayer in the Orthodox Liturgy which follows the words of institution: 'Remembering . . . all that for our sakes was brought to pass, the Cross and tomb, the Resurrection the third day, the Ascension into heaven, the sitting on the right hand, *the coming again the second time in glory. . .*' (my italics). I owe this point to Bishop Basil Osborne.

yourself in the presence of God'. What the books do not make very clear – but anyone who has seriously tried to pray will – is that this involves putting yourself in the presence of the present, i.e. trying to put away the distraction that pulls you away from the experience of this body and this mind in this moment into some sort of fantasy, some chain of self-consoling thought. It is so easy, however, to misunderstand what is going on in the process of settling into the prayer of stillness. You can run away with the idea that what is required is rigorously to abstract yourself from everything that is actually going on in your mind and body, to try to force your mind to a Somewhere Else that is the realm of piety and holiness. In fact, the beginning of stillness is a patient attention to where you are and to what is going on within you. Observe the rhythms of your heart and breath; try to look at or to name the preoccupations, fears, desires, that are around in your mind and heart; feel the texture of the chair or the floor. Arrive. The hardest thing in the world, they say, is to be where you are.

The odd thing is that this takes us back to the classical and early Christian conviction that contemplation is a confrontation with God as simple 'being'. Greek-speaking Christians (and Jews) translated the 'I am who I am' of Exodus as 'I am the One who is' – as an affirmation of God's transcendent, independent existence. Some moderns have complained that this reduces the 'dynamic' language of the Hebrew Bible to a philosophical concept, but this is too crude a criticism. The Greek vision is precisely of a divine life that needs no 'maintenance' from outside itself, that is free from the conditioning of any particular reality. What is distinctive about the Jewish and Christian reading of this is simply that the freedom of God is grasped as fully shown in certain events and transactions in our world: in the liberation of the Hebrew slaves; in the human life and death of Jesus.

We have seen earlier in this chapter just how this vision comes painfully to light in the trial of Jesus as Mark narrates it. To understand and appropriate the transcendence of God is to see that Jesus' affirmation of his unbreakable rootedness in the life of God, precisely at the moment when no worldly condition secures or makes sense of this, is the fullest historical testimony there could be to what his divinity involves. Every believer drawn into the same 'obstinate uselessness' of witness thereby speaks effectively of who Jesus is.

Mark's story may be like a film in its rapidity, and like a modern work of fiction in its evocation of a world without real sense, yet strangely it points us into silence and stillness before its central figure. The trial establishes that in Jesus there is to be discerned the still point of the world, needing no justification, no security beyond itself. Whenever we are free enough to move away from justification and security, to move away from the whole process of trying to make sense of it all for ourselves in our own terms, we are – whether we know it or not – accepting the verdict passed on our world by Mark's Jesus.

Questions for reflection and discussion

1 How have you coped with times of feeling helpless, or times when what you do does not seem to have any meaning?

2 In what ways do you think Jesus has been misunderstood in the life of the Church?

3 What are the pictures that most readily come to mind when you try to think of God's greatness or transcendence? And what experiences have brought home to you something of that greatness?

4 Where have you seen examples of people carrying on because of their faith and their love, even when it seems useless in the world's eyes?

5 Is God supposed to make us feel safe?

Prayer

Jesus,
hold our minds still,
keep us from running off into the past or the future,
so that we can meet you where we are —
in happiness or in grief,
in confidence or in anxiety,
in life and in death.
Amen.

CHAPTER TWO

Matthew: Wisdom in Exile

Making connections

At his trial Mark's Jesus breaks the silence and the secrecy that has surrounded his mission throughout the narrative. Matthew's Jesus does not have the same silence to break. The Jesus of this Gospel sometimes echoes the language of Mark in forbidding those healed by him to talk about it (e.g. 8:4; 9:30), but he can equally *encourage* people to speak of what they have heard and seen, as in the pivotal episode in Chapter 11 where Jesus addresses the followers of John the Baptist, appealing to his great works as an answer to the question of whether he is the one who is to come: 'The blind see again, and the lame walk, lepers are cleansed, and the deaf hear, and the dead are raised to life and the Good News is proclaimed to the poor' (v. 5). Unlike Mark, Matthew is concerned to show that the Spirit of God is fully active in Jesus in the ways the prophets promised (see also 13:28, on the Spirit at work in the casting out of demons). There is something there to be recognized, something that makes sense because of what is already known.

Matthew is also generally rather kinder to the disciples than Mark, on the assumption that they have the capacity to see what there is to see, even though their fidelity to the vision is not much more impressive than it is in Mark (Peter still has his rebuke from Jesus, straight after an even more solemn commendation of his faith than we find in Mark). When Jesus asks the Twelve, at the end of the longish series of parables in Chapter 13, 'Have you understood all this?' they reply, 'Yes.' Mark would have loaded such an episode with irony; Matthew simply goes on to report Jesus' saying about the function of learned scribes who become learners in the kingdom of heaven and are able to deploy both the new wisdom and the old.

This verse (13:52) has often been seen by commentators as something of a summary of Matthew's own concerns, perhaps even an indication of his own background as an expert in the old wisdom who has become a pupil in the new kingdom. This may be rather fanciful (Matthew does not exactly come across as an *expert* in Jewish matters), but it does bring into focus a very important aspect of the Gospel. It is about *understanding*, about picking up clues and seeing whole what most people only see in fragments. The parables Matthew records are about seeing the whole picture. How tempting it is to look at short-term results, to grab at quick solutions that fail to grasp how time itself reveals the truth. How bizarre seem the actions of someone who sells all their property in order to buy a patch of unpromising meadowland – unless you happen to know about the buried treasure. Matthew, you might feel, would have appreciated Sherlock Holmes:

> **I took the tattered object in my hands and turned it over rather ruefully . . .**
>
> **'I can see nothing,' said I, handing it back to my friend.**

> 'On the contrary, Watson, you can see everything.
> You fail, however, to reason from what you see. You
> are too timid in drawing your inferences.'[1]

One of the frequent delights of the Sherlock Holmes stories is to see the great detective doing something apparently utterly absurd. We know that there must be some stunningly good reason for his actions, and we do not suppose, as Watson so often does, that Holmes' mind is finally giving way. There is something to see, but our sight is not yet educated enough. Matthew is not in the business of Holmesian deduction, but there is an inescapable affinity with the stories in the way Matthew scatters clues and allusions and, like Holmes with Watson, delights in making the connections we missed, even though they were there all along, just waiting to be spotted.

A perfect example of this is Matthew's love of referring to the Hebrew Scriptures. This or that episode in the story should call to mind for us this or that text from the Scriptures. All along the way, those around Jesus should have been able to pick up what the story was really about in the light of these connections. The family tree of Jesus in the first chapter is a famous example of 'Holmesian' exposition. Here is a record of apparently impressive ancestry, interrupted four times by allusion to unimpressive or disreputable outsiders – namely the women, Tamar, Rahab, Ruth and Bathsheba, either foreign, immoral or both. Now consider the scandal around Mary's unexplained pregnancy. Does anything suggest itself to you? At the very least, you may conclude that human scandal

---

1 Arthur Conan Doyle, 'The Adventure of the Blue Carbuncle', *The Adventures of Sherlock Holmes*, in *The Penguin Complete Sherlock Holmes*, London: Penguin, 1981, p. 246.

is no disproof of God's hand at work. At most, you will see that the interruption of orderly patriarchal succession in the family of David and Abraham is, paradoxically, part of the continuity of God's work. You may also appreciate the point (still a problem for unimaginative readers) of the concluding, enormous divine joke: this is not a family tree at all, because Mary's child is of God, not of Joseph the son of David. The family history was preparing us for a paradox, if only we had known how to read it.

If only we had known how to read it: the *pathos* of Matthew's Gospel lies in this. The cues and the clues are given, but those who know them do not respond. Jesus says,

> 'What description can I find for this generation? It is like children shouting to each other as they sit in the market place:
> "We played the pipes for you,
> and you wouldn't dance;
> We sang dirges,
> and you wouldn't be mourners."'
>
> (Matthew 11:16–17)

This comment reflects the underlying darkness of Matthew's apparently orderly mental world. Yes, the connections are there, and yes, there can be a delight in spelling them out for those who will not see what is there; but in the actual context of Jesus' life, the incomprehension is shadowed more and more with danger. God's order and ours do not dovetail as neatly as we should like.

God's Wisdom – the hidden unity

Matthew, as scholars like to remind us, is a theologian of God's Wisdom – wisdom in the sense defined by those passages in the Old Testament and the Apocrypha, in Proverbs and Job, Ecclesiasticus and the Wisdom of Solomon that celebrate creation as a reflection of and a sharing in the joyful order and coherence of the mind of God. The passage quoted above leads into the enigmatic claim that 'wisdom has been proved right by her actions' or 'by her children' (v. 19). Those who are adopted into the family and fellowship of God's Wisdom will be able to see the coherence of the world, to see how the bizarre and the incongruous may yet be God's self-communication. What about those who continue to make themselves strangers to Wisdom, however? One recent discussion of Matthew on Wisdom has pointed out very acutely that the passages most clearly identifying Jesus with Wisdom itself, especially in this highly significant eleventh chapter of the Gospel, are precisely those that stress the inclusiveness of Jesus' work. Due to the full presence of divine Sophia (Wisdom) in Jesus, 'membership within a patriarchal family is dramatically replaced by membership within the family of disciples gathered around Wisdom . . . and the metaphors used for this discipleship are inclusive – brother and sister and mother (12:46–50)'.[2] Refusal of Wisdom is a refusal of this inclusive vision; refusal of Wisdom is going to be, ultimately, an act of violence against what seems incongruous and discontinuous – even though it is in truth the hidden logic, the hidden unity, of the world.

2 Elaine Wainwright, 'The Gospel of Matthew', in Elisabeth Schussler Fiorenza (ed.), *Searching the Scriptures: A Feminist Commentary*, London: SCM Press, 1995, p. 654.

Much more could be said of Matthew's strategy as a whole in the Gospel, but these are the salient points. It is a narrative of hidden harmonies displayed, of disparities overcome by pointing to some extraordinary and unexpected analogy between the words and events of sacred history and the events of Jesus' life. It is therefore an appeal to the reader to learn how to look, how to 'scan' the ambiguous world so as to read what it is truly saying. It is centred upon the belief that the identity of Jesus is what finally gives coherence to the history of God's dealings with his people – i.e. that he *is* Wisdom. It also prepares us gradually for a rejection of that Wisdom, which will show itself as a climactic moment of exclusion, an exclusion which will also be a *self*-destruction.

The questioner questioned

In the light of all this, let us now turn to the trial story itself. Commentators have sometimes been puzzled by the fact that Matthew 'weakens' Jesus' response to the High Priest's challenge, 'Tell us if you are the Christ, the Son of God.' In place of Mark's bold statement, 'I am', we have the verbal shrug of '*su eipas*', 'so you say', or 'the words are your own' (26:64). Matthew generally makes far less than Mark does of the necessary secrecy about Jesus' identity, so why the apparent evasion here? The answer lies in what we have been looking at in terms of the structure of the whole Gospel. The High Priest is using words drawn from the history of his people. Does he know, Jesus asks, what those words might actually mean? It is almost as if Jesus says, 'It's for you to tell me whether I am what you think I claim to be. The world in which these words about God's anointed make sense is *your* world.'

Of course there is something here of Mark: these words, the words of the accusation, are not in themselves the truth, any more than any of the words the world may use will tell us finally who Jesus is. But the extra edge in Matthew is the turning of the question back upon the questioner. It may remind us of Jesus' response to the sons of Zebedee when they ask for places of honour in the kingdom. 'Do you know what you are asking?' he says on that occasion (Matthew 20:22; Mark 10:38). Or it may call to mind the exchange with the religious leaders over the authority of Jesus and John the Baptist (Matthew 21:23–7; Mark 11:27–33): how *do* you know where to recognize divine authority? Jesus' answer to the High Priest at his trial has a twofold force: you *know* how to look at the world, you already have the categories to make sense of it; but you use these categories as if you had *no understanding* of what they might truly mean.

This trial turns out to involve putting to the proof an entire system of religious language, at least as it is spoken by these people in this situation. What do words like 'God' and 'anointed' mean in the mouth of the High Priest, presiding at such a tribunal? If he knew what he was saying, would he not either fall silent at once or realize the answer to his question? Jesus' question is this: 'Do you know yourself, your history? Do you really *inhabit* the words and the forms you use so fluently?' The High Priest speaks for a history in which Wisdom is inscribed, the human story that is Wisdom's story. Turn back to the Wisdom of Solomon in Jewish Scripture, and you can see how the biblical record is reworked as the record of what Wisdom has done to and through human agents.[3] The High

3 See in particular Chapters 10 and 11 of the Wisdom of Solomon.

Priest's question, rooted as it is in his people's story, shows how the story has become dead in his mouth, dead in the hands of those who now claim power among God's people. The power represented by Caiaphas, in its urgent anxiety to exclude and destroy Jesus, has become a power that excludes Wisdom itself.

Misplaced blame

This is where we have to tread very carefully, because it is the elaboration of something akin to this insight that has made Matthew's Gospel the tool of the most corrupt and murderous misreading of the passion stories that has disfigured the Church's record. Matthew, as the modern reader cannot forget, makes the crowd outside Pilate's palace shout, 'His blood be on us and on our children!' (27:25). The evangelist's bitterness at the schism within God's people that continues in his own day, his impatience with the refusal of the Jewish majority to accept the preaching of Jesus, overflows into this symbolic self-denunciation by 'the people'. It is all too likely that his first readers heard it as a corporate acknowledgement of guilt by the Jewish nation, and that they connected it, as do other New Testament writers, with the devastation of the nation and its sacred place in the terrible disasters of AD 70, when the Romans destroyed the Temple and along with it the last vestiges of independent power for the people. Read at this level, it can only make the contemporary Christian think of all the centuries in which Jewish guilt formed so significant a part of Christian self-understanding, and of the nightmare which was made possible by this in the twentieth century.

As we read this against the background of the trial scene, however, we may see how its point can be felt not as an assault against certain guilty 'others' but as a question to religious power and religious fluency, a question to all who are *insiders*, all who are familiar with speaking about God and God's Wisdom. If Matthew meant the cry of the crowd as a simple acceptance of guilt by the whole Jewish nation, then his own trial story might suggest that *he* has not seen what Jesus' verdict really is. In terms of the reading of the answer to Caiaphas proposed above, the only possible sense that can be given to the words, 'His blood be on us,' is that it is an implicit admission by the managers of religious power that their exclusion of Jesus is a refusal of their own life and wholeness. In the liturgical reading of the passion as it is now practised in churches, the crowd's part is normally taken by the whole congregation together – certainly an acknowledgement of what the Holy Week liturgy often reinforces, i.e. that the only example that matters in the worship of an unfaithful and rebellious people is us, the present worshipping body. It might not be a bad idea, however, for this to be spoken by the clergy, in acknowledgement of the particular role Matthew gives to those who act as guardians of the history and integrity of the people.

Our fear of the truth

Those who are under condemnation in Matthew's narrative are ultimately those who have the story of God's Wisdom written in their common life, but who cannot read this story because they do not know themselves. By a roundabout route, Matthew returns us to Mark: what we think we are sure of, the language we speak so familiarly, is at odds with the truth. If we were to encounter directly what we talk about so freely, we should be terrified, angry and murderous. Once again, H.F.M. Prescott's story about the sixteenth-century English Reformation presses home the point. About halfway through the narrative, Malle, a serving maid at Marrick Priory who is universally regarded as halfwitted, sees Jesus. We see him too, through her eyes, for a few unforgettable pages, as he makes his way through the convent and village as a travelling workman. Christabel the Prioress sees him too, but without recognizing him. He is 'an ugly vagabond knave' in her eyes and she feels 'strangely and strongly moved against the fellow'.[4] Later, when she believes for a moment that Malle's vision might after all be used to help save her beloved convent (and her own authority), she tries to extract from the servant something that will reinforce her longings, but finds that she does not know what or how to ask.

> 'What . .?' the Prioress began, and must stop to clear her throat. It came to her with a shock that now she feared to be told what the woman had seen . . . But she drove off the fear; what else but good should God, Our Lady and Saint Andrew intend to their servants? Yet she knew that of that good she was as much afraid as if God were her enemy.'[5]

Christabel is not a monster. One of the great achievements of the novel is to make us feel for her, cold and harsh as she is. And one of the things that keeps the reader's sympathy is

4 Prescott, *The Man on a Donkey*, p. 402.
5 Ibid., pp. 412–13.

precisely the few moments when she is vulnerable to the truth, when she cannot deny the complexity of her feelings and her knowledge, at some fairly well-buried level, that she is working consistently against God. They may be moments instantly overridden and denied, but they have not become impossible. This encounter with Malle is one such. Christabel remains that little bit sympathetic because she speaks to the fear that any moderately sensitive believer will experience with more or less regularity. What if I became incapable of telling truth from falsehood? What if the maintenance of my religious identity became a weapon against God?

It is not an infrequent theme in the literature of belief and doubt. Kazantzakis's turbulent and somewhat overheated work of fiction, *Christ Recrucified*,[6] shows us a Greek village preparing for a passion play. Inexorably, the Gospel events begin to play themselves out in the lives of the actors, especially when the village is challenged to welcome an influx of refugees. When Manolios, who is to play Christ in the drama, takes the side of the refugees, the powers that be in the village have him killed, with the parish priest taking a leading role in the plot. Somehow, however, this dramatizes the Gospel conflict in excessively colourful terms. Christabel and Malle come closer to the experience of most of us, for whom the decisions are not, in the Kazantzakis style, issues that are instantly and obviously ones of life and death, but are rather gnawing anxieties about whom to believe and how to put the right questions to ourselves.

6 Sometimes called *The Greek Passion*, first English translation published New York: Simon and Schuster and London: Faber, 1953.

Christ and self-understanding

The truth is that we do not know in advance how we might react, which in turn suggests that we are never in a position to identify those 'others' who are responsible for the killing of Christ so as to point a condemning finger. Matthew's narrative does not allow the believer – in particular the articulate and educated believer, the teacher, the expert – any fixed answer to the question of how I might know that I am still with Jesus rather than with Caiaphas. As soon as there seems to be an answer to such a question, it becomes part of just that system of religious words and religious fluency that helps to make possible the exclusion of Jesus. In the presence of Jesus at his trial, faith unavoidably takes on something of a catch-22 dimension. What matters is to *hold still* before the question.

Yes, of course we may discover specific acts, specific patterns of behaviour and speech that put us on the side of Caiaphas, and there are things we can do to change those and to make reparation. There is no escape, however, from the summons to be in the presence of Christ on trial. It is as if he said to each believer, 'Stand where I can see you,' and my faithfulness to him is going to be bound up with the whole diverse process of keeping myself 'in question'. This is not a matter of obsessional self-scrutiny, the search for an impossible transparency to my 'real' motives or desires. It is only a sober and consistent recognition that I have no final and satisfying account to give of myself, and must wait in Christ's presence to learn who I am. I must wait without the expectation of a tidy personality profile ever being provided, but in the hope that Christ's knowing of me will give me whatever wholeness I am capable of receiving.

The language of faith

Neither is this a recommendation to ignore the historic language of faith, the crystallization of Wisdom into words. The issue is not whether or not to look for words to express our faith (we cannot avoid doing that), nor is it whether or not the formulations of faith can lead to arrogance, exclusivism and self-satisfaction (obviously they can and do). It is more to do with what we expect the language of Christian doctrine to do, and in the light of what we have been thinking about here, the answer to that must be that the job of doctrine is to *hold us still* before Jesus. When that slips out of view, we begin instead to use this language to defend ourselves, to denigrate others, to control and correct – and then it becomes a problem.

A recognition of this inspired Dietrich Bonhoeffer's great challenge to 'religious' language in the meditation he wrote for his godson from prison in May 1944.

> Reconciliation and redemption, regeneration and
> the Holy Spirit, love of our enemies, cross and
> resurrection, life in Christ and Christian discipleship –
> all these things are so difficult and so remote that we
> hardly venture any more to speak of them. In the
> traditional words and acts we suspect that there may
> be something quite new and revolutionary, though we
> cannot as yet grasp or express it. That is our own fault.
> Our church, which has been fighting in these years
> only for its self-preservation, as though that were an
> end in itself, is incapable of taking the word of

reconciliation and redemption to mankind and the world.[7]

It is not that the words are mistaken, or that they are – in the glib modern sense – irrelevant, so that we need clearer and simpler ideas. Far from it. The problem lies in the speakers. There is not enough *depth* in us for the words to emerge as credible; they have become external to us, tokens we use while forgetting what profound and frightening differences in the human world they actually refer to. If the point of traditional doctrinal forms is to hold us still, it is also, we could say, to create a depth in us, a space for radical change in how we think of ourselves and how we act.

Use and misuse of language

It is true that a good deal of what earlier Christian generations took easily – or apparently easily – for granted now creates puzzles and uncertainties, or even just boredom. Here the Christian community faces a very complicated set of issues. If we proceed to revise and adjust so as to avoid any hint of difficulty, we are likely to find that we have ironed out much of what challenges us by its very strangeness; we leave no room for depth to be created. Yet if we try to ignore the gulfs in understanding and assumption, we make Christian language and doctrine once again a tool of power and self-defence.

This has recently been brought home to many most forcefully in relation to the unreflective, continuing use of

7 Dietrich Bonhoeffer, *Letters and Papers from Prison,* enlarged edition, London: SCM Press, 1971, pp. 399–400.

gender-exclusive language in theology and worship. It feels like another catch-22 situation. To be sensitive to these issues can lead us into such paralysing self-consciousness about our religious speech that it is never allowed to *work* for us, but becomes a means for the expression of negotiated and agreed human views. To refuse to be sensitive, to defend an uncritically pious use of the tradition, equally prevents the language from working, since it makes it the conscious preserve of one group defending its position against another. This particular stand-off goes a long way towards explaining why, in many modern disputes in theology and ethics, both 'right' and 'left' can give the impression of using the terms of their understanding more as weaponry than as invitations to stillness or to depth.

Perhaps there is no solution to this, no policy that will allow us simultaneously both proper self-awareness and contemplative perception. Nevertheless, it makes it all the more urgent to remind ourselves of what we are doing when we discuss theology or the language of worship, to be aware of what our expectations are. It becomes all the more vital to focus our attention on those words and images that still speak for what unites believers, what deals with their basic identities as renewed in Jesus. We do right to bring into critical light any expressions of this which reflect unexamined human power patterns (the example of gender-limited terms is, as I hinted just now, the most obvious example in the eyes of most). What we most need, however, is a certain distance from the underlying attitude which assumes that doctrinal statements are there first and foremost to assert a *position* which may be accepted or contested, like other positions – rather than being there to place us in a certain kind of relationship to truth, such that we can be changed by it.

If this means a greater degree of simplicity and reticence in the language of worship, that is all well and good, so long as the simplicity is not for the sake of removing what is strange to us. In a way, it is like the question of whether and how we should read the Bible in its entirety. We suffer from two equally unsatisfactory policies, on the one hand treating it with undifferentiated credulity and using it as a clincher for our arguments, on the other editing and improving it so as to make it less difficult. What we have to learn is surely the skill of allowing the words of the Bible the authority to bring us into the presence of God and to hold us there.

Freeing ourselves to see the truth

Let me put this a bit differently: the goal is that we should be set free from an attitude – however expressed – of *ownership* where the words and images of faith are concerned. We have been reflecting on the Gospel confrontation between those who see their task as the guardianship of God's Wisdom as it has been shown to them in their history and Wisdom herself. Part of the tragedy arises, perhaps, from the perennial tendency among religious people to forget precisely what it means for Wisdom to appear in history – as something unfolded in the unpredictabilities of the passage of time. Perhaps the temptation of Caiaphas is always to think of truth as present here and now, in a timeless finality that can be possessed by the religious institution. Whatever the truth of this may be, it is worth recalling how Matthew, throughout the Gospel, makes us see that the new perspective of Wisdom interrupts and reorganizes the landscape in ways that are not predictable – exactly as he does with the surprises hidden in the family tree of Chapter 1, as we saw earlier.

In turn this suggests that the ability to *recognize*, which is so crucial to living in Wisdom, is likely to show itself most clearly when connections are made between improbable things and persons (as in Chapter 1, once again, with the outrageous connections implied between the virginal Mary and the adulterous Bathsheba and her disreputable sisters). The most vivid instance of this, however, is probably the great parable of the sheep and the goats in Chapter 25. The king recognizes the just, even though they have not recognized him explicitly: what they have done is to recognize his claim and to act in Wisdom, feeding the hungry, welcoming strangers, visiting the sick. Those who know the criteria for recognizing Christ yet fail to apply them to the needy at their doors become unrecognizable to Christ himself.

Recognizing Christ

Father Dimitrii Klepinin was a Russian priest who, along with the famous Mother Maria Skobtsova, worked in Paris during the German occupation, providing French Jews with forged papers to assist their escape. Then he was captured.

> Fr Dimitrii was interrogated for four hours. He made no attempt to exculpate himself. Later, at Lourmel, Hofmann was to describe how he was offered his freedom on the condition that he helped no more Jews. Fr Dimitrii had raised his pectoral cross, shown the figure on it and asked, 'But do you know *this* Jew?' He was answered with a blow to the face.[8]

8 Sergei Hackel, *Pearl of Great Price: The Life of Mother Maria Skobtsova 1891–1945*, second edition, London: Darton, Longman and Todd, 1982, p. 120.

Both Mother Maria and Father Dimitrii died in the camps. Eyewitnesses recalled the way Father Dimitrii was mocked: 'One of the SS began to prod and beat him, calling him *Jude*.'[9] This is a densely significant pattern of recognition. The priest has absorbed Matthew's lesson as it is meant to be absorbed – there is no hint that he allowed some myth of corporate Jewish guilt to override his recognition that, in Paris in 1942, in the wake of the rounding-up of nearly 7,000 local Jews into the sports stadium on the Boulevard de Grenelle preparatory to deportation, '*this* Jew', the crucified Jesus, was to be found among the persecuted. His appeal to his (supposedly Christian) interrogators is an appeal for such a recognition to be shared. They know – they must know – this Jew at least. Then in the mockery Father Dimitrii meets as he is herded off to the camps himself, he in turn is recognized as a 'Jew', as someone who has, so to speak, earned the right to be counted with the crucified and with the Jewish kindred of the crucified.

If the symbol of the crucified does not make this sort of recognition (and this sort of *being* recognized) possible, it has become an empty sign. If it becomes simply a pious way of giving meaning to my own suffering; if it becomes a symbol of human pain in the abstract; if it draws attention because it speaks to our fascination with pain, it is no longer in any useful sense the cross of *Jesus*. If it becomes the badge of a group causing or colluding with the suffering of others, it is no longer the cross of Jesus. The American theologian George Lindbeck queried some years ago whether an armed crusader crying 'Christ is Lord' as he slaughtered Muslims could really

9 Ibid., p. 123.

be said to be making a true statement.[10] We might say that the words in the abstract represent the true state of affairs in the universe, but no words are ever used in the abstract. Yet again, we are brought back to the theme of our first chapter, the danger of familiar words about Jesus, and are reminded of the theme of this present chapter, that such familiar words may come to represent not what they are supposed to be about but the power of the speaker and the powerlessness of others.

Healing a broken world

In the mythology of classical Jewish mysticism, the *Shekhinah*, the presence of God, which is also identified with God's Wisdom, is fragmented in the creation of the world. Broken into scattered sparks of living truth, it is buried deep in the texture of the material order, hidden in the lives of surprising people. Some writers sketch a picture of God's Wisdom as a princess in rags, wandering through the world until God's people discover her and lead her home. Lives of holy wisdom are the way in which the brokenness of creation is mended – although the breaking will always, in this world, in this history, begin again. The saint brings together the *Shekhinah* above and the *Shekhinah* below, in one famous formulation, living a life that is so consistently open to God's presence that the glory of heaven shines fully through the splintered remnants of it in the world.

10 George Lindbeck, *The Nature of Doctrine: Religion and Theology in a Postliberal Age*, London: SPCK, 1984, p. 64. 'The crusader's battle cry "*Christus est Dominus*" [Christ is Lord], for example, is false when used to authorize cleaving the skull of the infidel.'

Basic to this haunting picture is the acknowledgement of the paradox that Matthew puts at the centre of his Gospel: Wisdom is the most fundamental reality in creation and in the history of God's people, and yet it is the hardest of all things to recognize. When it is recognized, healing becomes possible for the world's blind injustice and violence. Jesus on trial for his life before the supreme judge and teacher of the covenant people is a concrete image of the *Shekhinah* broken and exiled, royalty in the dress of a beggar. If we follow through the logic of the trial, we may see that recognizing Wisdom in the dress of a beggar – quite literally, as Matthew 25 reminds us, recognizing Wisdom's summons in the specific needs of the powerless – requires us to become familiar with some kinds of dispossession, some kind of letting go. The Wisdom that lives in the life of Jesus is Wisdom exposed to the pain and insecurity of human life in the world; to live in and by this Wisdom means a willingness to endure with Jesus and to follow his self-emptying in whatever way we can. In the particular context of the trial in Matthew, it means letting go of whatever it is that allows us to use the language of faith as a defence or a weapon.

Attuning ourselves to God

In his *Confessions* (VII, 18) St Augustine describes his condition before his final conversion as one in which he could not see what lesson Christ's weakness had to teach, or how 'your Wisdom, through whom you created all things, might become for us the milk adapted to our infancy'. 'Not yet,' he goes on, 'was I humble enough to grasp the humble Jesus as my God.' 'Humility' is a word with negative overtones for most moderns, but the point Augustine makes here is as contemporary as ever. It is not that Wisdom is discovered by blind submission and self-denigration – although the history of the Church might often suggest that. It is rather that his previous search for Wisdom by strenuous abstraction from the material world and its history of struggle and sin is shown to be misguided.

Wisdom speaks through the weakness of a human life: only by accepting my own weakness, and surrendering various comforting falsehoods that might let me think myself strong and safe, can I attune my life to that of God. The goal is not to create the spurious weakness of deliberate self-denigration, nor is it a policy of avoiding conflict by pretending to a sense of one's own worthlessness. Augustine is not talking about *worth* here, but about the inescapable contradictions and vulnerability of actual human life. What deceives us about these things is what keeps us from truth, the living truth that is in Christ's human birth and life and death.

To put it in rather different and more technical terms, God's Wisdom is 'kenotic'.[11] It defines itself in the self-forgetting, self-emptying love of Christ, the eternal Word, who lives a human life for our sake and is obedient to the point of death. Such Wisdom will always be an exile, a refugee, in a world constrained by endless struggles for advantage, where success lies always in establishing your position at the expense of another's. The first step in acquiring God's Wisdom is therefore to search for what one recent writer has called 'the

---

11 'Kenosis' is the word used to describe Christ's voluntary surrender of certain divine characteristics, in order to identify himself with humanity. It comes from the Greek word *kenos*, meaning 'empty'.

intelligence of the victim'[12]– not because it is good or holy in itself to be a victim, far from it, but because looking at the world from the point of view of those excluded by its systems of power frees us from the need always to be securing our own power at all costs. The victim is the person left over or left out after a system has done its job, and is therefore an abiding challenge to the claim of any system to give a comprehensive solution to human needs and problems.

Standing with the victim means adopting a questioning stance towards such claims. In addition, as we try to move to where Jesus stands at his trial, we are challenged to listen to what we ourselves are saying. We use the language of God's unconditional love, of God's action submitting itself to be worked out in the history of weak and sinful people, of God's Wisdom made flesh in the pain and failure of Jesus' death. 'The words are your own,' says Jesus. If you mean them, where do you stand?

Questions for reflection and discussion

1 Looking back at your life, do you see continuities across experiences that felt at the time like huge changes and ruptures?

2 Can you think of a time when a familiar word or picture in worship 'came alive' for you in unexpected ways?

12 See James Alison, *Knowing Jesus*, London: SPCK, 1993; and *The Joy of Being Wrong: Original Sin through Easter Eyes*, New York: Crossroad, 1998, especially Chapter 5.

3 Do you remember any occasion when your understanding of what it means to be a Christian was challenged or shaken by an unexpected person?

4 How would you react if someone you knew claimed to have had a vision of Jesus?

5 Does saying the Creed in church feel at all like exploring something? Or does it feel more as if you and the rest of the congregation are just going through the motions?

Prayer

Jesus,
help us not to hide in our churchy words;
when we worship, let us know and feel that there is
    always something new,
something fresh to see of you.
Do not let us forget that you will always have more to
    give us,
more than we could ever guess.
Amen.

CHAPTER THREE

Luke: Knocking on the Window

Outside the boundaries

> Standing in the rain,
> Knocking on the window,
> Knocking on the window on a Christmas Day.
> There he is again,
> Knocking on the window,
> Knocking on the window in the same old way.

Sydney Carter's song brilliantly weaves together the biblical image of Christ standing at the door and knocking (as in Revelation 3:20) with the everyday picture of someone arriving at the door with a hard-luck story, with perhaps just a hint of carol singers at Christmas too, bringing a message no one wants to hear.

> No use knocking at the window.
> There is nothing we can do, sir.
> All our beds are booked already,
> There is nothing left for you, sir. . .

No, we haven't got a manger.
No, we haven't got a stable.
We are Christian men and women –
Always willing, never able.[1]

At the end of the last chapter, we were thinking about 'the intelligence of the victim' – the perspective that can only belong to those who are excluded from the organizing systems of their world. Luke is particularly interested in this perspective. It is often said that Luke is a Gospel aimed at the non-Jewish world, but this is only a half-truth. It is far more accurate to say that it is a Gospel aimed at the world of those who do not belong, be they Jews, Gentiles or whoever, and that, from the very first chapter, Luke is out to question our ideas about where the centre of things lies, so as to question the way we draw our boundaries.

In the first three chapters of the Gospel, Luke deliberately sets the scene by giving us a point of reference in secular history: 'In the days of King Herod of Judaea' (1:5); 'Now at this time Caesar Augustus issued a decree' (2:1); 'In the fifteenth year of Tiberius Caesar's reign' (3:1). These are the ways in which the world draws its maps, with the crowned head at the centre of things, the world organized around his presence and measured by his history. In each of these chapters, however, the story immediately turns to a figure or figures conspicuously on the edge of things – a childless, ageing couple, an unmarried village woman, an eccentric in the desert. The characters around them are just as marginal:

1 Sydney Carter, 'Knocking on the Window', © TRO Essex Music Ltd.

shepherds, who were not regarded by the religious purists as capable of fulfilling the Law's full demands, or the strange and lonely figures of Simeon and Anna in the Temple. In Chapter 3, John the Baptist speaks contemptuously to the devout children of Abraham and kindly to the tax collectors and the soldiers. The heroes of these stories are outsiders on several counts. They are either outside the 'normal' structures of solid, patriarchal or tribal life because they are childless, widowed or unmarried, or they are the sort of people who are not expected to be able to manage behaviour that is pleasing to God.

A change in perspective

These are the people who are involved in God's activity – the 'poor', not in the sense simply of those who are economically deprived, but those who have no expectations or at least low expectations, those from whom others look for little or nothing, those without a clear visible 'stake' in the larger world they occupy. They are lifted up by a God who snubs and turns away the powerful. In what is happening to them a light is dawning that will change the perception of all people. The three great hymns of these chapters, the songs of Mary, Zechariah and Simeon, all turn on these themes: God has honoured the promise once made to the chosen nation; God has turned upside down the assumptions of the world; God's light has dawned for Jew and Gentile alike in this great intervention.

The story that then unfolds after the opening of Chapter 3 is, naturally, a story of the act of God among outsiders, and it is given force and point as Luke leads us through the successive confrontations of Jesus and his followers with

the representatives of Herod and Caesar. In his Gospel and in
the Acts of the Apostles which follows, Luke has more trial
scenes than the other evangelists, simply because he is determined to tell Jesus' story in and through the experience of the
disciples as well. The points of orientation at the beginning of
the Gospel, the solemnly invoked figures of Herod, Augustus,
Tiberius, Pilate, Annas, Caiaphas and the magnificently
obscure Lysanias of Abilene (does Luke – just a little – have his
tongue in his cheek by this point?), are in various ways
brought into contact with Jesus and his disciples. Jesus' off-
hand remark about Herod Antipas (13:31–3) and his brief
and silent appearance before him on trial, the testimony of
Peter and John in Acts before the priestly courts, Peter's arrest
by another member of Herod's family, Paul's appeal to Caesar
– all these can be seen as Luke's reinforcement of the pattern
set down in the opening scenes of the Gospel. He pinpoints
events like these to remind us that the whole story is one in
which the human map is being redrawn, the world turned
upside down (see Acts 17:6).

In the course of the Gospel itself, the theme is also explored
more gently, even poignantly – through the parables of loss,
humiliation and welcome (the prodigal son, the Pharisee and
the tax collector) and through the incidents where Jesus in
some local encounter changes the perspective, shifts attention
from what seems to be the centre of things. In Chapter 7, for
example, the sinful woman who intrudes upon the Pharisee's
dinner party becomes the focal figure; in Chapter 19, with a
faintly comic effect, Zacchaeus, who hoped to avoid being
noticed, finds all eyes fixed on him when the Lord addresses
him. Those who have no assurance of their *right* to a welcome
or a hearing are those who turn out to be the most welcome.

People without a voice

In Luke's version of the parable of the great feast (14:15–24), the emphasis is not so much on the invitation being extended to good and bad alike (as in Matthew's version), but on the helpless, those who expect nothing or can take no initiative for themselves. Very significantly, it follows immediately after Jesus' advice not to ask to dinner those who can be relied on to return your hospitality (14:12–14). What has to be broken down is an entire pattern of calculating human worth in any system of exchange – this or that person is worth taking seriously because of their status, their virtue, their ability to play their part in the particular game going on. Here too the connection is clear with the opening chapters: Zechariah, Mary, Simeon and Anna are not productive contributors to their social world, they are not people who slot easily into a role in the central matter of the continuance of clan and nation.

What does it mean to be without the right to a hearing, without access to the currency of the prevailing market? It is to be without words, to be without the ways in which those around you tame and organize the world. Your own language does not count – whether literally, in the case of subject people whose language has no legal status, or more broadly, when the whole shape of the speech of those in power reminds you constantly that your perspective is not included. You cannot speak in a way that will actually make a difference; your coinage is rejected; nothing you say will 'come out right', will persuade or succeed. This is why, in Luke's account of the trial before the High Priest, the themes already explored in relation to Mark and Matthew are given a new colouring. In Luke 22:67, Jesus is asked by the council to tell them if he is the Messiah. "'If I tell you,' he replied, "you will not believe me, and if I question you, you will not answer.'" In other words: I have nothing to say to you that you will be able to hear or to which you will be able to respond. Luke's Jesus places himself with those whose language cannot be heard.

Luke thus nudges the reader back towards Mark's picture yet again. Where and what is the 'transcendence' of God? For Mark, it is visible in the lonely protest, the decision to do what is truthful, in spite of the absence of any 'useful' outcome. Luke takes us a step further, and it is a bold step: God's transcendence is in some sense present in and with those who do not have a voice, in and with those without power to affect their world, in and with those believed to have *lost* any right they might have had in the world. God is not with them because they are naturally virtuous, or because they are martyrs; he is simply there *in* the fact that they are 'left over' when the social and moral score is added up by the managers of social and moral behaviour. Or, to put it a bit differently, God appears in and through the fact that our ways of arranging the world always leave someone's interest, welfare or reality out of account. We cannot organize our world so as to leave everyone a possible place. We are unavoidably bound to exclusion as we try to give form to our social and moral life.

A God of connections

Does this mean, then, that God is a sort of vast moral dustbin, offering to all the unquestioning affirmation that human beings cannot give, sweeping aside all issues of ethics, all considerations of responsibility in the life of a community? Or are we committed to claiming some kind of moral superiority for 'outsiders' simply by virtue of them being outsiders? Both of these are natural reactions from the conformist mentality that always identifies God with existing forms of power and belonging, but both are equally mistaken. Luke is as clear as any other Christian writer that there are human actions that do and human actions that do not align with the actions of God, that there are judgements to make, decisions to work out and kinds of behaviour that fall under condemnation. Nowhere does he suggest that there is something superior about the outsider as such. Zechariah really is a prosaic and timid country cleric; the woman at the Pharisee's house really is a sinner; Zacchaeus really is a greedy collaborator. The difficult thing for the reader, ancient or modern, is setting aside both the idea that God has no character and no claims and the idea that God's 'morality' is that of the rebel, the loner, the person who lives in an atmosphere of moral risk and mental drama, or of the victim, the one who suffers defeat and loss.

So what is Luke telling us through the way he positions God with the outsider? In an important sense, he is not saying anything about right and wrong. If we thought that God was to be found in and with the outsider because God approved of them more than he approved of insiders, we should be falling back into just the mentality we are being urged to forget. We should end up looking at outsiders for signs of the sort of thing of which God would approve, and replacing one set of standards for belonging with another. This is always the irony in movements of rebellion – the creation of new conventions to express an absolute freedom from the old ones, the identifying of new heroes to replace the old role models. Those who

grew up in the 1960s will be familiar with some of the con-
formity that rebellion can create. A counterculture is no less a
culture because it rejects one set of conventions in favour of
another.

No, Luke's point is in a way much simpler than this. One
modern writer has said that God is in the connections we
cannot make, and that tells us something of what is on view
here. The person who is 'left over', whose place I cannot
guarantee, whose welfare I cannot secure, who does not fit, is
the person who reminds me of my own limits; and as I
acknowledge the incomplete character of my world of reference and my understanding, I may at least see the seriousness
of the question about the fate of those not catered for. If in
any sense I recognize a claim of care for such people, even if
I have no idea how to effect it, I am at least some way towards
perceiving how God lies in the connections I cannot make.

Allowing the rights of others

All systems, moral and social, begin with the sense that my
own understanding of my desires and needs is not the whole
story. Yet it seems that all such systems end up by discounting
or giving up on certain others. What starts with the recognition that the other has real claims just as I do always seems to
end with certain claims being put 'on hold'. Most frequently,
in political visions, the claim of certain kinds of people to
welfare or happiness in the present is indefinitely suspended
for the sake of the future. Classical Marxism and modern
capitalism have this at least in common: starvation now –
but justice tomorrow; unemployment now – but a property-
owning democracy tomorrow.

This is woven into so much of our thinking today, in terms of insoluble conflicts of 'rights'. The convicted killer who has changed and grown radically over the 20 years he has spent in jail has a right, we might say, to a new start. Oh, but then the parents of a murdered child have a right – don't they? – to know that the outrage that destroyed their lives is not forgotten or absolved. Whatever decision is taken, the effect is to create an outsider, someone who has no leverage, no moral currency, in the new situation. Also, more prosaically and immediately, what are we to say of the unfinished business in our own lives, the people we shall never be able to 'make it up to'? Those who have never forgiven me, or whom I have never forgiven – they are the outsiders in my biography, the ones whose absence and nonreconciliation spoil the satisfying outline of my life.

Sometimes our most well-meaning efforts to avoid making someone an outsider will only reinforce the problem. They take for granted that the way we manage things is right and normal, and try to tell other people that they can and should manage in just the same way. There are some searching words on this in a recent book of stories and reflections from the East End of London, stories of various people who have been involved in one way or another with the Franciscan house at 42 Balaam Street in Plaistow. These are extraordinary stories by people who have, for the most part, little experience of being 'insiders' in any system that guarantees influence or gives you a voice in the wider society. The stories are moving, funny and mostly – in the strict sense – quite pointless. That is, they are not out to illustrate anything or prove anything, but simply to be themselves.

Telling stories is not everything, however. Towards the end of the book, the editor Deborah Padfield includes a brief section on 'unspoken stories', the stories of those who cannot find or do not want the kind of speech that most of the book represents. They include refugees from cultures where issues of privacy and sharing are experienced differently, or from countries where any critical words spoken abroad would put lives and liberties in danger back home. Deborah writes:

> It is easy for me, middle class westerner, to assume that it's good to talk, that to know more of each other is to understand more. 'Sometimes,' comes the answer. Silence is as valid as speech: each have their place. And knowledge of each other is not lightly gained . . . And communication demands effort also of the listener. 'Why do these things, that to me have so little significance, matter so much to you?' Once ask that question and a lifetime of enquiry opens up, into worlds as subtle as they are complex and private, guarded against heavy-footed outsiders.[2]

'The story is never complete,' she concludes, 'but it acts as a signal, reminding us of the wholeness which cannot be told but which is there, often mutilated . . . yet unique.'[3] The whole of this book is a remarkable example of letting God make the connections that we cannot. It does not aim to persuade or to shape all this diverse experience into an argument for this or that. There are stories about homelessness, about poverty,

2 Deborah Padfield (ed.), *Hidden Lives: Stories from the East End by the People of 42 Balaam Street*, London: Eastside Community Heritage, 1999, pp. 143–4.
3 Ibid., p. 144.

about the experience of life as an immigrant or a refugee, about homosexuality, about old age and loss – but no campaign is being fought. You would have to listen very hard to the particularities of the stories before you decided what, if anything, you thought should be done. The main thing is the listening itself, with all the sense of incompleteness that goes with it. Here is a story full of gaps and silences. Here is a set of experiences that does not fit any programme or support any conclusion. Here, to quote Deborah again, the silences 'challenge the listener and her world: what am I, what kind of assumptions mould me, that this person should fear my response?'[4]

Dealing with 'otherness'

Reflections like these testify to how difficult it can be to resist the passion to bring someone into your own world, your own language – and how necessary it is to respect the silence of another, even when (or especially when) it unsettles your own hopes of completing the picture. The American theologian Stanley Hauerwas gives a further turn to this point in one of his excellent discussions of the role in the Church of those we call 'handicapped', those with severe physical or mental impairments. The question posed for the majority of us by such people, he says, is more than merely an issue of securing 'better treatment' for the impaired. 'The true moral question is what kind of community ought we to be so that we can welcome and care for the other in our midst without that "otherness" being used to justify discrimination.'[5]

4 Ibid.
5 Stanley Hauerwas, 'The Moral Challenge of the Handicapped', in *Suffering Presence: Theological Reflections on Medicine, the Mentally Handicapped and the Church*, Edinburgh: T. & T. Clark, 1988, p. 185.

More specifically, he suggests, the question posed by the handicapped is related to 'the larger question of the place of children in our lives'.[6] Children both are and are not 'members' in our society (and our church communities). They are unavoidably there, but their involvement and responsibility are not the same as an adult's. So they are tolerated primarily as 'potential adults', with the unspoken assumption that there is something wrong with being a child. Now if, as regularly happens, those suffering impairments of various kinds are treated as children in society and in church communities, the problem is obviously that they are *not* going to grow out of it. They are frozen in a state that is tacitly regarded as substandard, but with no possible escape.

What is needed, Hauerwas suggests (although he acknowledges that there are no direct solutions to this), is a greater critical awareness of the problems both in how we regard children and in the assumption that the handicapped person is essentially a child, needing the kind of protection a child might require from the consequences of their actions, and so being denied the maturing risks of ordinary adulthood. The point is reinforced when we think about the baffled and even angry reactions that are provoked when 'the handicapped' protest about their treatment and demand more freedom to determine their living conditions. We are hurt and bewildered because – surely? – we have been doing our best to look after them.

6 Ibid.

Learning to enlarge our world

Here is the moment when the challenge of Luke's Gospel – and Luke's trial – becomes concrete. We are faced with someone who cannot speak our language. Do we retreat, perhaps even with impatience and anger at the fact that this someone will not co-operate? Or do we allow ourselves to be taught something about our own incompleteness? Frances Young, introducing a collection of essays and reflections about the experience of the L'Arche communities, touches briefly on this in connection with her experience of relating to her own son, who has severe mental and physical impairments:

> I have to say that to describe my son as having learning difficulties is meaningless: I have learning difficulties myself – I've never felt so incompetent as the evening I spent in a L'Arche *foyer* almost unable to make myself understood because of my inability to express myself adequately in French. But there was that other L'Arche *foyer* where language was irrelevant – as it is with my son. He has made me competent, through years of practice, in non-verbal communication.[7]

To see that I have 'learning difficulties', that my usual mode of coping *cannot* cope with this experience, this person, is to allow the stranger to go on being the stranger, rather than becoming a failed member of my world or an incompetent speaker of my language. Then to be taught by that stranger is to allow that

7 Frances Young (ed.), *Encounter with Mystery: Reflections on L'Arche and Living with Disability*, London: Darton, Longman and Todd, 1997, Introduction, p. xiii.

my world can be enlarged in ways beyond my plan and control – precisely through the recognition that the stranger really is a stranger. To conscript the other into my own frame of reference is to commit one sort of mistake; to refuse to listen or learn because they are 'strange' is another.

The stranger here is neither the failed or stupid native speaker, nor someone so terrifyingly alien that I cannot even entertain the thought of learning from them. They represent the fact that I have growing to do, not necessarily into anything like an identity with them, but at least into a world where there may be more of a sense of its being a world we *share*. Recognizing the other as other without the immediate impulse to make them the same involves recognizing the incompleteness of the world I think I can manage and moving into the world which I may not be able to manage so well, but which has more depth of reality. And that must be to move closer to God.

Space for children

We have been thinking about one particular kind of otherness, that of the people we call handicapped (a word that rapidly tells us what most of us think is the important fact about them, and which therefore already expresses the problem of our limited world). In his reflections on people living with impairments Hauerwas also touches on that kind of otherness embodied in childhood, and he rightly observes that our culture has become more and more impatient with childhood as a state in itself. We hustle children into pseudo-adult roles and choices as soon as we decently can, or rather sooner than we *decently* can – especially through the systematic assault on the child as possible consumer which is represented by modern advertising of toys and leisure goods. Although this looks like provision for children's needs or wants *as* children, the truth is that it creates habits and expectations that assimilate the child into the most obsessional adult purchaser.[8]

Nonetheless, it will not do for Christians to take too quickly to the moral high ground where children are concerned. Not only is the child in church still an embarrassment and a nuisance for many congregations, but there is also a deeper issue, explored with all his usual depth by the late Donald Nicholl in an essay about the places where theology has been and is carried out.[9] His basic question is, 'Who is *not* expected to be around in the places where theology is thought and written?' Historically, one answer to that has been 'women', and Christians are still catching up with the effects of that exclusion. Less obviously and equally importantly, however, we would have to say 'children' as well. Given that Jesus had strong comments to make about attending to children and recommended that his followers should imitate children, there is something very odd about a Christian discourse that ignores the child. 'How can you live in accordance with the teaching about being children if you are for ever hiding yourself away from children?' asks Nicholl, and he argues that this reinforces the need for theology to be done in the kind of human community 'where men and women are together, and . . . where children are not hidden away'.[10]

8 For further thoughts on this matter, see Rowan Williams, *Lost Icons: Reflections on Cultural Bereavement*, Edinburgh: T. & T. Clark, 2000, Chapter 1.
9 Donald Nicholl, 'Is there a *locus classicus* for theology?', in *The Beatitude of Truth: Reflections of a Lifetime*, London: Darton, Longman and Todd, 1997, pp. 52–64.
10 Ibid., p. 62.

Moral short-sightedness

Once we have started, of course, the list of the excluded swells
quite rapidly. Children and the disabled, yes; and what about
the nonhuman world, the way in which we ignore or override
its integrity and otherness on the assumption that our story of
human needs and priorities is *the* story of the globe? Yet even
when we start taking seriously the moral reality of this nonhuman world, we need to remain aware that it can become
another source of moral short-sightedness. It is strange, for
example, to find passionate advocates of the rights of the nonhuman creation, defenders of the rights of animals, among
the ranks of those who do not seem to think that abortion is
an issue where 'rights' conflict. If we are trying to listen to
those who are defined out of our normal systems, it must
surely be imperative to keep the unborn human in our view.

Confusingly, this principle cuts across the conventional
left–right divides in our ethical squabbles. Abortion is often
seen as a 'right wing' concern, and – for example – homosexual rights as a 'left wing' one. But there are parallels, in that
those who define themselves as homosexual represent yet
again an 'otherness' that will not go away and cannot be readily accommodated into the world of the majority. If that is so,
then God must be listened to here as well. Elizabeth
Templeton has put it starkly, contrasting what she calls the
ethics of earth and the 'ethics or non-ethics' of heaven:
inevitably, we seek order, because order limits pain and fear
for most of us, but we must beware of identifying this with
the law of God without remainder. 'We dare not identify God
with these norms. For if there is one person on earth who
is, by such ethics, devalued, dehumanized, demonized or

disqualified from the conversation towards truth, whether that be on the grounds of sexual behaviour or any other, then I believe we lie, and possibly blaspheme.'[11]

The important expression here is perhaps 'the conversation towards truth'. Conversation may or may not lead to conversion in the sense of one party adopting the viewpoint of the other, and if we only conversed when that was our aim, we should experience nothing but very tense and polarized communication in this world. As I said above, it is not that the outsider is by definition right, nice or superior, but simply that the outsider's very presence puts a question that reminds me that my account of things, my way of making the world all right and manageable, is not only an incomplete enterprise, but may be an enterprise that is keeping out God because it lets in the subtle temptation to treat my perspective *as if it were* God's.

When we say that we must grow into the 'intelligence of the victim' as a way of aligning ourselves with the Wisdom of God, it means that our understanding of the environment in which we live has to grow into the freedom to see things from the viewpoint of the excluded and, beyond that, to grow together into an understanding that neither the insider nor the outsider can yet imagine. Conversation is the only way of even beginning on this road, not because of any simple liberal convictions about the goodness of dialogue or because of any hope of a tidy, negotiated solution, but because conversation assumes that I shall in some degree change because of the other – not by becoming the same, but simply by entering a larger world.

11 Elizabeth Templeton, *The Strangeness of God*, London: Arthur James, 1993, p. 117.

Seeing beyond our limitations

Returning to Luke, and particularly to his opening chapters, we can see how he is effectively saying that Herod, Augustus and Lysanias of Abilene all inhabit a *smaller* world than the 'poor' of the Gospel narrative – the old cleric, the pregnant girl, the field labourers, the eccentrics in the Temple. If Jesus says to the priestly court that he does not know how to speak to them in words they can understand, this signifies that his world is larger, not smaller, than theirs. His helplessness is part of the poverty of all the excluded, but it is also like the 'poverty' of a poet trying to explain how he or she works, or the 'poverty' of a Daniel Barenboim trying to explain to the eight-year-old practising for a Grade 1 violin exam what it is like to play an instrument as if it were an extension of yourself, or the 'poverty' of an Andrew Wiles trying to articulate why a particular mathematical problem can engage your mind in delight, passion and frustration for decades.[12]

These daunting reaches of art and science are also, in our world, reminders of both otherness and limitation. They do prompt us, however, to see more clearly that the language in which the world is routinely managed can be a language with its own desperate poverty and triviality. The challenge is whether, when we are confronted in our general human dealings with the outsider, the person or perspective left over, we can sense in this experience something of the same troubled awe we may feel in the presence of art or higher mathematics. This child, this adult with cerebral palsy, this member of another race, this man or woman whose experience is so alien

12 See Simon Singh, *Fermat's Last Theorem*, London: Fourth Estate, 1997.

to mine, this strange physical environment, can address me as surely as Barenboim or Wiles might do, reminding me of the constraints of the world in which I have made all too comfortable a home. This takes us back to a point made in my first chapter: the whole idea of *transcendence* is somehow being refashioned as we reflect on Jesus' trial. For Luke, the transcendent is bound up not just with the lonely witness facing failure but also with the voiceless and powerless of this world.

The pain of powerlessness

Another way of putting this is to say that we are in most danger when we deny our own poverty or neediness, and that the presence of the powerless is painful in large part because they reconnect us with that unwelcome need. They do not live in the world we like to think we live in, the world we can organize, so they tell us that our world is smaller than we thought. At its most extreme, this perception can lead to violence: the poor must be eliminated or at the very least pushed right out of sight, because they make us uncomfortable. Herod, Augustus and Lysanias are threatened by the knocking on the window. The police break up a nonviolent demonstration with water cannon. The homeless must be rounded up and swept off the streets before the VIP's visit.

For Christians it is therefore extraordinarily important, radically important, to live in a context where we are not protected from the visibility of the powerless. The witness of L'Arche again speaks to this concern. Jean Vanier writes of his own experience after relinquishing the leadership of the network and simply living alongside one particular disturbed young adult, finding in himself deep deposits of anger and pain when faced with the screaming of this young man: 'If I had been alone with him, not in community, I could have been tempted to hit him. I was terribly humiliated by my attitudes,' he comments. But, he continues,

> Could Jesus be hidden in my own darkness, I wondered? I began to discover how the light of God is called to enter into darkness, that I must not hide or deny this darkness to myself or to others, pretending that I am part of an elite ... How could I really accept the woundedness of Antonio or Peter if I was not accepting my own?[13]

Looking at this problem in a more familiar context, one of the commonest experiences for anyone bringing up a child is the sense of helplessness and radical failure of control when that child will not go to sleep. For many parents – as I can testify with feeling – this is an experience that helps them understand a little of why truly desperate parents eventually resort to violence against their children. There is absolutely nothing that will reassure you that you are in control, because you are not; perhaps all you can do to convince yourself that you can change the situation is to act violently. This is a terrible situation for anyone and, thank God, for most of us there are all kinds of inhibitions and self-monitorings that come into play, perhaps even a recognition of what is really going on, an understanding of the passion to prove that you have not lost control. Nevertheless, when we look at the world at large, how very clear it is that there are also countless subtle

13 Jean Vanier, 'L'Arche – a place of communion and pain', in Young (ed.), *Encounter with Mystery*, pp. 10–11.

disguises for this resort to violence, and all because we cannot otherwise persuade ourselves that we are not powerless.

The threat of Jesus

It is not surprising, therefore, that in all the Gospel narratives of the trial, Jesus' declaration of the gulf between his world and that of his judges provokes insult and abuse. He is beaten, flogged and crowned with thorns precisely *because* he is powerless: because he is powerless, because he does not compete for the same space that his judges and captors are defending, he is a deeper threat than any direct rival. He threatens because he does not compete (again raising the question of what transcendence really is), and because it is that whole world of rivalry and defence which is in question. Luke adds one very specific irony to the story with his reference to the new alliance between Herod and Pilate which comes about as a result of the trial. The judges of Jesus have more in common with each other than with him; the competitors for space in this world are bound together in what has been called the 'mimetic' trap – we imitate our enemies, we want what they want (and we want them not to have it when we do), and so human conflict is fought out in a hall of mirrors.

Mark's account of the trial makes us think about the difference of Jesus in terms of God's alienation from almost all our language of meaning, let alone success. In this court, we are being cross-examined on our readiness to reduce God to a provider of meaning and usefulness in the terms with which *we* are comfortable. Matthew's trial probes the degree to which our religious fluency blocks out the divine Wisdom, and it begins to ask us what we make of those who are left out or left over by the systems we inhabit. Luke takes us a step further and challenges us not only to stand with those left out and left over, but to find *in ourselves* the poverty and exclusion we fear and run away from in others – to find in ourselves the tax collector in the Temple, the woman in Simon's house, and both the sons in the parable of the prodigal, with their different kinds of exclusion, guilt or fear.

Confronting our own frailties

Ultimately, the knocking on the window, as Jean Vanier reminds us, comes from inside as well as outside, from the left-over elements in each of us, stirred and revived so uncomfortably by the presence of the poor, the voiceless, the uncontrollable – from the crying child to the master musician to the uncountable millions who suffer incurably and anonymously in the famines and wars of our age. This in turn suggests the thought that when Jesus tells his followers to become like children, one of the things he may be exhorting them (and us) to do is to name and confront our own inner regions of helplessness and speechlessness. Luke's court examines us on our fear of ourselves, our fear of our own silences and weaknesses.

The truth about Jesus which the courts seek becomes more and more obviously something that raises the question of how we are going to be truthful about ourselves. This truth that we do not want to confront in turn appears more and more obviously as something to do with our fear of a sort of homelessness: we need to inhabit a territory that is clearly defined and capable of being defended. We need to know where we are. This is not an evil in itself, but as we reflect on the gulf between Jesus and his judges, it seems that, left to ourselves, we will see this as a test of our power to dominate our environment. Somewhere – we would like to believe – there exists the possibility of being 'at home' without this costly struggle for a defended territory. What would it mean for us to live in the truth so habitually that we were genuinely at home with all our frailties and poverties? What would the truth be that could be experienced as *hospitable* in such a way?

Questions for reflection and discussion

1 Who are the important people in your 'map' of the world in which you live?

2 As you look at the community in which you live, who is it who does not have a voice, a presence, an influence? Who needs listening to?

3 How does your church community react to people seen as 'handicapped'?

4 How does your church community make children feel at home – or does it not do this?

5 Can you think of any experiences you have had when you have been served and helped by someone you had not expected would have anything to give you?

Prayer

Jesus,
you welcomed people,
and you let them welcome you.
Let me have the same hospitality to others,
and the same grace to accept what they give me.
Thank you for making the whole world welcome
in your Father's house.
Amen.

CHAPTER FOUR

John: Home and Away

The challenge of identity

You could read the whole of John's Gospel as a trial story. Again and again, Jesus is exposed to hostile questioning; again and again, he struggles to bring to light the suspicion or unbelief that prompts such questioning, to position himself against the self-referring and self-sufficient categories of his questioners, and to redefine where they stand and who they are. Written – evidently – at a time of savage bitterness between the community which the Gospel addresses and the parent community of the synagogue, this positioning and redefining reads painfully today, because the history of the Gospel's reception includes so much of that anti-Jewish passion that disgraces and disfigures Christian identity. It is as if John's concern is always to define Jesus as what 'the Jews' are not, and therefore to define Jewishness as opposition to truth or reality – and it is only a short step from there to the startling and frightening moment in 1 Thessalonians where the writer calls the Jews 'enemies of the whole human race' (2:15).

Nothing is going to make this easier for us, but, as with the similar problems in Matthew's Gospel, we have to attend to the deeper rhythms of John's exposition rather than turn away in disgust. If we do turn away, we miss the point – again as in Matthew – about how our assumptions regarding our own 'believing' identity are put into question. Repeatedly, John's theme is that those who consciously identify themselves as the ones who really believe or really know are also those who cannot bear the light that comes from Christ; and those who identify themselves as Abraham's children, children of election and promise, prove unable to live in the trust Abraham showed. The fundamental issue is to do with the challenge to the 'insider', just as much as in Luke. That challenge comes not because of new teaching or new information, but because of who Jesus is. John, like other New Testament writers, is in fact clear enough that Jesus' identity as child of Abraham and David is precisely what gives a tragic edge to the constant misrecognitions or refusals to understand that run through the narrative.

A question of authority

In this respect, it is interesting that John spends relatively little time on Jesus' trial – or at least interrogation – before the High Priest. The short episode in which Jesus is questioned by Annas, the patriarch of the high-priestly family, seems almost specifically designed to show the irrelevance of any issues about Jesus' teaching at this point in the story. Jesus' reply to Annas' questions about his doctrine and his disciples is dismissive: he is basically saying, 'You should know *that* by now' (see 18:20ff). We, the readers, should also certainly know that by now, and this is not going to be an investigation to establish any kind of neutral record of Jesus' career. As his response after he has been struck by the High Priest's servant suggests, the ground of hostility cannot lie merely in what has been *said*. It is left to Pilate to ask the crucial questions.

It is, incidentally, plain that 'the Jews' in the story of the trial before Pilate are not a rabble or a popular assembly, as in the other Gospels, but representatives of the priestly caste – a small but significant qualification to any over-rapid assumption that John is concerned simply to demonize the nation as a whole. Equally, we should be cautious about assuming that John is out to give us a favourable picture of Pilate, in contrast to a damning picture of the Jewish people. On the contrary, Pilate appears as weak and petulant, finally acting against his convictions to secure his threatened place in the imperial favour. Anne Wroe, in her wonderful study of Pilate's character in Scripture and legend, has it right when she comments on Pilate's extraordinary words, 'Take him yourselves and crucify him' (John 19:6). This is, she writes,

> . . . a ridiculous thing to say. I find him innocent, but yes, kill him. Your immorality and illegality are fine with me. I'm only a Roman judge, what do I know? Or even more ridiculous: *You* crucify him. The Jews could not crucify anyone. He meant, if you are so keen to kill him, go ahead. Don't make me do it. Like so much that day, it came out idiotic and wrong. Even his insults didn't work: his anger and his flippancy alike evaporated uselessly above the seething heads.[1]

1 Anne Wroe, *Pilate: The Biography of an Invented Man*, London: Jonathan Cape, 1999, p. 252.

It is Pilate, not Caiaphas, who is left with the job of putting the question that cannot be answered in the language in which it is asked: 'What is truth?' he asks (18:38), the most celebrated question in the whole of the New Testament. It is part of an interrogation whose focus is, very explicitly, *authority*. Is Jesus a king? If he is, whose king is he? If he is, how are we to imagine an authority that is not conceived in ethnic or political terms? What *is* authority outside such terms?

Pilate has begun by asking Jesus if he is a king, and Jesus has answered that his royal authority is not the world's kind, 'not from hence' in the old translation – i.e., either 'not derived from this world order' or 'not of this sort', the sort where people fight to defend a territory. Both possible meanings are significant. Jesus' royal character is independent of legitimacy, succession, or any external assurance that he is the rightful heir. The kingship he exercises is the kind of power that cannot (not should not, but *cannot*) be defended by violence. Pilate's puzzled, 'So you are a king then?' (18:37) draws from Jesus the same response he makes in Matthew and Luke to the High Priest: '*Su eipas*' – 'It is you who say it.' To talk of 'kingship' is to use the limited language of imperial administration. Use the word if you must, but remember that its content is utterly changed. This kind of royal authority is inseparable from the task, the calling, of embodying truth. The rule exercised by this kingship is simply the recognition by others that the truth thus embodied compels their attention, their listening. If you cannot give any meaning to this ('Truth? What is that?'), there is no more to be said.

Truth as freedom

It is a definition of authority as a particular kind of freedom. We are left asking how it is that a life might be so open to truth, so open to how things ultimately are, that it has such compelling authority over other lives. We are also left asking what makes *us* so unfree and so untrue in contrast. Earlier in the Gospel Jesus promises, 'If you make my word your home you will indeed be my disciples, you will learn the truth and the truth will make you free'(8:31–2). Thus, if listening to the words and acts of Jesus becomes the environment in which you live, you will discover the freedom to be drawn ever deeper into truth. And – as the passage in Chapter 8 goes on to develop the dispute with a Jewish audience over their descent from Abraham – the implication is that 'making your home' in any other atmosphere is what makes sin and violence possible. If your 'home' is a confidence in the status secured by race or power, you are not free and so not truthful, and therefore a prey to those temptations that drive people to violence.

We may catch echoes here of Mark's governing theme: what makes us secure in the world's terms is the enemy of the transcendent God. John, however, has a good deal more to say in definition of this liberating truth that spells out, as Mark does not, something of what it means to be grasped by it, to be vulnerable to it. In so doing, he begins to answer the question posed at the end of the last chapter about how truth can be experienced as 'hospitable' and can free us to live without the unceasing struggle for territory.

The theme of truth occurs several times in the 'farewell discourses' of John Chapters 14–17, and the reader of the dialogue with Pilate will have been alerted already to the resonances of Jesus' self-definition there by the model of truth sketched out in these earlier chapters. Truth is associated with the Spirit, the 'Advocate' (15:26; 16:13) – Jesus sends the Spirit who comes from the Father as one who will stand alongside, accompany and defend believers, and this accompanying and defending is a journey into 'complete truth' (16:13). Living in the truth is a 'consecration', a making holy, which is once again associated with receiving and abiding in the 'word' spoken through Jesus, and this leads on to the climactic point in John 17 when Jesus promises that his friends will be where he is, seeing him as he truly is and receiving the Father's love without reserve.

Living in truth means living where Jesus lives. In the farewell discourses, the shadow of the passion of Jesus constantly shows on the horizon, and it is obviously part of being where Jesus is that the believer shares in Jesus' vulnerability and death. Jesus' friends will be hated as he is hated. When Jesus speaks of being 'consecrated in the truth', the reader is immediately invited to connect this with Jesus' 'consecration' of himself, which can only mean the death he is to endure. Truth and death are brought together with alarming closeness: truthful living is the full acceptance of the real and concrete danger of pursuing faithfulness in this world; it is an acceptance of risk and mortality. It is also a letting go of what denies such mortality, what deceives us into believing that faith will not put us at risk – literally at risk of persecution and death, and more widely at risk of losing those securities and defences which tame the God we worship in Christ. There is a more positive dimension, however, in the promise of being able to share Jesus' vision of the Father and his relation to the Father. Seeing truly means seeing the glory given to

Jesus by the Father (17:24), and in some sense sharing that gift (and being commissioned to share it, to make it visible, in turn).

Unthinkable violence

Now if we turn from the farewell discourses back to the scene before Pilate in Chapter 19, a number of things come into clearer focus. Jesus says to Pilate that if his kingship were the kind the world is used to, his followers would fight to prevent his capture. However, because it is not this kind of authority, defensive violence is useless, unthinkable. If Jesus' followers fought to prevent his betrayal and death, they would be fighting against Jesus himself, the Jesus who has so consecrated himself that he will use nothing to defend, justify or secure himself. To surround him with violence is to try to make him what he is not. Towards the end of H.F.M. Prescott's *Man on a Donkey*, as the doomed rebels wait bitterly for their execution, Malle the serving maid sits by the Thames in the shadow of the Tower of London, seeing 'darkness, and God moving nigh-hand in the darkness'.

> 'Man,' said Malle, 'would take swords, bows and bills to save Him. And the angels wait to break Heaven and let burning justice and the naked spirit flake down in flame to heat to scorched souls those men that bear God to die, so that they may know their Maker.
> 'But he will not ... There He is, and holdeth in His hands that glass vessel, clear, precious, brimmed full with clean righteousness. So He hath carried it without spilling, through life and now through death...

> 'Ah!' she cried, 'stay them! Stay them! lest with
> their swords they shatter the glass, and so the water is
> spilled, for we need it every drop.'
> She looked at Wat, and he cowered away. 'Sword
> cannot save righteousness – only spill it for the
> thirsty ground to drink. And that He knoweth.'[2]

Above in the Tower, Thomas, Lord Darcy, the tough old sol-
dier who has reluctantly been drawn into the rebellion and
now sits under sentence of death, lets his anger flare for a
moment against his confessor: not only has the rebellion
failed because of treachery and incompetence, but the clergy
have failed to summon the people to resistance and so have
betrayed their own cause, for which others must now die. Yet
the old friar tells him that this is not God's way. What other
way is there? Only the foolishness of God.

> Darcy did not move or speak for a long time. At last
> he raised his head and the friar saw something that
> was almost a smile on his face. 'Well,' said my Lord
> lightly, but as men speak lightly before a last, hopeless
> fight, 'I am not of so holy a mind as to be able to take
> God's way. But,' he said, and met the friar's eyes, 'I'll
> not grudge to die. It may be He will accept that for
> service.'[3]

Darcy cannot bring himself to be – as he sees it – a passive
martyr and is, like most of us, anguished by the cost of
failure. Nonetheless, he does what he can and embraces his

2 Prescott, *The Man on a Donkey*, p. 740.
3 Ibid., pp. 741–2.

unavoidable death with the kind of acceptance that makes it an *action*, not a matter of fate. Clearly, we are meant to see it as indeed a 'service', and somewhere behind it is the recognition that violence, with its inbuilt trend to look for victory at all costs, is surely a shattering of the fragile vessel of truth. As soon as we begin to feel driven to defend Christ by the calculations of the world, by those tactics that inevitably make winners and losers, something is broken.

Legitimate defence?

Near the end of *The City of God*, Augustine puts before his readers a paradox worthy of Zen Buddhism. The only causes you can fight for, he says, are the ones that are not absolute; once you decide that what you are fighting for is absolute, you have made it relative.[4] Presumably, what this is about is the recognition that conflict is not something we can simply avoid in human society. It may be right to use skill and energy in defending this or that position within the overall strategy of our lives; it may be right to calculate where lesser evils lie and what actions may be justified, if not exactly 'just'. Augustine famously applied the lesson to war, which may be a defensible project in certain very closely defined circumstances, but can never be an undertaking directly in accord with God's holy will. Identify what you are defending with God's will, and you may be sure that you have driven a deep wedge between your cause and God. You have mingled *your* passion and fear with a witness to God's truth.

4 St Augustine, *The City of God*, Book XXII, Chapter 6, discusses the question of whether it could be legitimate to defend a state by betraying an alliance, and concludes that this could be justified only if the highest good were simply to continue in being in this world.

If there are things that become untrue when they are said (as we saw in Chapter 1), there are also, for Augustine, things that become untrue when they are defended, or at least defended in a certain way. For those of us not directly concerned with decisions about war, the application must be to how we regard the conflicts of our daily work and relations. When I am criticized, do I assume that my critic is deliberately sinning against the light? When my proposal fails or is delayed, how far will I go to see that it is finally successful? How much loss and suffering for others as well as myself am I going to 'budget' for? Do I actually believe that truth will ultimately look after itself, that it is still *there* on the far side of any controversy?

Guaranteed frustration

This is not a recipe for idleness or for a self-protective indifference, but a question about where we shall find ourselves when we have expended every reasonable effort and all that remains is a strategy (in international affairs, in personal relations, in Church politics) that begins to alter the whole tenor of what we are talking about, what we care about. To pick up a powerful phrase from a book on Mary by an American missionary in Africa, we have to ask who and what our grief serves.[5] At what point do we find that we are in fact willing to forget what we most deeply desire so that we shall not have to feel frustrated? If that is what happens, our intensity of feeling – whether grief, anger or some other emotion – will be serving not the object of our longing but a need in us not to feel

5 See Peter Daino, *Mary, Mother of Sorrows, Mother of Defiance*, Maryknoll, NY: Orbis Books, 1993, pp. 29, 42.

denied and unsuccessful. It will actually be a mark of our readiness to forego the reality of desire itself.

So we are faced with the sobering fact that desire for the truth will not spare us frustration. On the contrary, it will guarantee frustration, an acute sense of painful limitation, because it turns resolutely away from the satisfaction that the mind can manufacture for itself. We are touching on an enormous topic here, but it is worth noting in passing that this phenomenon – of struggle and frustration in our desire for truth and our efforts in language to do justice to it – suggests that it will not do to think that language is a self-contained system, or that we can ignore the question of how it relates to a reality which is there before it and beyond it. We are most definitely not able to show what such a relation might look like: we cannot get out of our skins. Yet we need to come to terms with the way language itself seems to insist that it is not simply playful and inventive, and with the reality of wrestling to find the best (or least ridiculous) way of articulating our response to what we stumble up against in our world.

Learning to 'be at home'

So far, nearly all of what has been said about 'living in the truth' has been to do with cost and struggle – living in the riskiness of Jesus' presence, where no external guarantee can establish that living there is the right place to be. We can recognize that this has to do with freedom, certainly, but it is not so easy to see that it has anything to do with 'hospitality', to pick up a word used earlier in this chapter and at the end of the last. In fact, the entire point of talking in this way about freedom, even about the risk of being where Jesus is and the austerity of what truth asks from us – the restlessness and refusal of gratification – is to underline an implication that is not far from the surface of John's narrative.

If the kingdom of which Jesus is king is a kingdom that cannot be defended against rivals, a kingdom that is radically undermined by the use of violence, it is a kingdom that does not compete for space in the world. The company of those who stand with Jesus is not a rival to other comparable systems (as we saw in Chapter 1); it simply is what it is. In that sense, of course, it is more threatening to those systems than anything that is just another competitor, because it puts into question the very definitions of belonging and power that previously seemed so obvious. It also warns us against thinking that what 'belongs' to Jesus is *territory* in the world of human thought, feeling, hope, etc., a part, great or small, of that common worldly territory over which we compulsively argue as human beings.

Thus the believer standing where Jesus stands is not someone who can only be 'at home' in a specific bit of this worldly territory. He or she has become a person at home everywhere and nowhere. If our considerations of the struggle and frustration involved in living in the truth might lead to the conclusion that such a life was marked by endless tension, dissatisfaction with the present moment and the present time, this is a crucial point of correction. We are not – it seems – permitted to be at home in the sense that we can feel ultimately satisfied with where and what we are, longing to hold on to it and unwilling to respond to challenge; we are not to settle down in our place and our time because we feel comfortable. There are always questions to be asked by us and of us. That said, however, what is asked of us is a commitment to the here and now – our questioning can never be an attempt to deny or to escape the present moment. To know this moment, this place, this body, this set of memories, this situation, for what it truly is and to accept this as reality, the reality with which God at each new instant begins to work: this is the 'being at home' we have to learn.

Living honestly in the present

This applies on many levels. You might think, for example, of the paradoxes of the healing ministry. Prayer seeks change, prayer expresses the conviction that pain or disablement is not in accord with God's purpose, yet a spirituality of healing that encourages us to say, 'This is not me, this is not real,' about our situation is deeply dangerous. As anyone who has had any involvement in this should be well aware, the recognition and acceptance of the material reality of injury, disability or trauma is the beginning of a restoration of that inner image of oneself as an integral system without which no serious healing can occur; and what follows from this in terms of organic change is a good deal less important. A spirituality of denial or a spirituality that insists on the transformative power of the will and imagination over the suffering body is liable simply to increase anger and guilt.

The same applies to any project for change or reform. I long for the Church to be more truly itself, and for me this involves changing its stance on war, sex, investment and many other difficult matters. I believe in all conscience that my questions and my disagreements are all of God. Yet I must also learn to live in and attend to the reality of the Church *as it is*, to do the prosaic things that can be and must be done now and to work at my relations now with the people who will not listen to me or those like me – because what God asks of me is not to live in the ideal future but to live with honesty and attentiveness in the present, i.e., to be at home.

What if the project in question is myself, and not some larger social question such as war? At the end of the day, it is the central concern for most of us. We long to change and to grow, and we are rightly suspicious of those who are pleased with the way they are and cannot seem to conceive of changing any further. Yet the torture of trying to push away and overcome what we currently are or have been, the bitter self-contempt of knowing what we lack, the postponement of joy and peace because we cannot love ourselves now – these are not the building blocks for effective change. We constantly try to start from somewhere other than where we are. Truthful living involves being at home with ourselves, not complacently but patiently, recognizing that what we are today, at this moment, is sufficiently loved and valued by God to be the material with which he will work, and that the longed-for transformation will not come by refusing the love and the value that is simply *there* in the present moment.

So we come back, by a longish detour, to the point to which Mark's narrative brought us: the contemplative enterprise of being where we are and refusing the lure of a fantasized future more compliant to our will, more satisfying in the image of ourselves that it permits. Living in the truth, in the sense in which John's Gospel gives it, involves the same sober attention to what is there – to the body, the chair, the floor, the voice we hear, the face we see – with all the unsatisfactoriness that this brings. Yet this is what it means to live in that kingdom where Jesus rules, the kingdom that has no frontiers to be defended. Our immersion in the present moment which is God's delivers the world to us – and that world is not the perfect and fully achieved thing we might imagine, but the divided and difficult world we actually inhabit. Only, by the grace of this living in the truth, we are able to say to it at least an echo of the 'yes' that God says, to accept as God accepts.

Understanding the world

This is a reminder of the complex way in which John speaks about 'the world' in his Gospel. The world is what is foreign to the truth, what hates Jesus and his friends, what Jesus declines to pray for, the source of violence and falsity. The world is also what God made and loves and what Jesus saves and brings to life. It is not easy to tease out what all this means, but it seems to be something like this. The world as a thing in itself, the world as a source of value, is always bound to various sorts of untruthfulness. As a thing in itself, it defines itself in contrast to its maker: it is the system, the order, of defence and competition; its untruthfulness is the all-pervasive myth that the otherness of God is a threat to its integrity and safety.

This fear of God's otherness means that the world fears and hates whatever speaks of that other source of value – it hates Jesus and the community of Jesus because they do not live by the same fears and do not use the same defences. The community lives in Jesus, and in Jesus the otherness of God is not separate from the loving gaze of the Father who gives everything to the Son. The community, living in the trinitarian life, sees God's mystery and difference entirely in terms of an eternal and unreserved self-giving. Jesus, acting out on earth that eternal gift which is the source of his being, continues the act of self-giving so that the creation may believe and

live. God loves the world because that is God's nature –
self-bestowal, self-sharing. The world's refusal and non-
recognition of this establishes the boundary that makes the
world an enclosed system hostile to God and hostile to anyone
who does not play by the rules of rivalry. Nonetheless, Jesus'
friends are not to be taken out of the world (17:15). They have
to live daily with those systems of hostility and competition.
In the midst of this, however, they know the world as it really
is, as God sees it, as the object of a love that is beyond violence
and rivalry. They inhabit that kingdom which has no defences,
the kingdom which does not derive from the world.

Christian 'unworldliness' is in fact a way of saying 'yes' to the
world by refusing the world's own skewed and destructive
account of itself. Christian faith refuses to accept that the only
alternatives are those the systems around them can recognize.
However, since we are caught up so much in those systems ourselves, we cannot always see such alternatives clearly, and we live
in an atmosphere of compromises and repentance. Yet we will
not settle for the options set before us by the world's managers
as the only things possible. We maintain a stubborn trust that
humanity could do its business in other ways and, by telling ourselves the gospel story and remembering stories of the gospel
taking effect in other people's lives, we keep that trust vivid and
concrete. We accept and acknowledge where we are and we
recognize that we shall only see the world and the present
circumstances of our lives with clarity and truthfulness if we
step back from the world's habitual ways of making sense. The
Christian task, in the middle of all these struggles and failures, is
to try and see situations without the colouring of these worldly
habits, to see them fresh, to see the flesh and blood of the
moment, not the ideologies that draw our gaze away.

Tuning out reality

The hardest thing in the world is to be where we are. We sur-round ourselves with devices for not seeing – increasingly so, ironically, as we acquire better means of information. We theorize, justify and theologize; we search for perspectives that will make particular and personal problems less painful; we describe and redescribe experiences so that we shall not have to sense them quite so rawly; we invite into our minds such a profusion of images that we can be confident no single one of them will lodge deeply enough to be really disturbing. The news begins with a flood in Bangladesh or the murder of schoolchildren, but we move on quickly – 'And now the rest of the news . . .' – and we are safe with the adventures of a delinquent politician and a controversial award in the enter-tainment industry. After the news there is another programme to look forward to anyway.

This is how it is, and so far from guaranteeing that we are aware of what is currently going on in the world, we end up with no clear apprehension at all of a real present moment. It is wonderfully easy to persuade ourselves that knowing about a lot of things is the same as entering into their reality and even making a difference. No. 'Being where we are' requires a formidable amount of switching off – of those very systems and stimuli that purport to make sense of the environment.

Here is the 'hospitality' of truth we began to think about at the end of the last chapter. To let go of the habitual patterns of understanding so as to allow ourselves to be anchored in this moment, confident that this is where God is to be met – that is to be welcomed by truth, to enter into that place (or non-place) beyond territories and defences. Letting go of what gets in the way of this is terrifying at times and deeply costly. It is also the only possible way for us to receive unconditional joy – not happiness, but joy, the sense of fundamental attunement to reality. John's Jesus, after all, prays on the eve of his final (and foreseen) torture that his *joy* may be in his disciples and may be as complete as can be.

The joy which is his can only be the awareness of being held absolutely in the gaze of the Father, receiving moment by moment the completeness of his love. Jesus has no defences before that loving source of his being, and he therefore communicates without reserve or interruption the hospitality of the divine life, which seeks to keep nothing back. 'Everything the Father has is mine' (16:15). To hear and recognize what Jesus is saying, doing and suffering is to recognize the God whose nature it is to give life, who eternally 'makes room' in the divine life for the loving exchange between the divine persons and who, out of that fulfilled mutual delight, makes room for his creation within the realm of divine joy.

Seeing the world whole

To be in the truth of Jesus, to belong to his kingdom, is to be on the road to seeing the world whole, seeing the world with the eyes of God. This is a never-to-be-finished undertaking, but one that can judge and shape what we do from day to day, that will open us to those passing glimpses of full vision that assure us we are not just living a fantasy. St Benedict, we are told, near the end of his life saw the world 'as if gathered into a point'. Julian of Norwich famously saw the world in its wholeness held in Christ's hand like a hazelnut. In Thomas Keneally's blackly comic novel about Australian Catholic life in the early sixties, *Three Cheers for the Paraclete*, the sceptical priest Maitland has to sit on a panel examining a young nun for alleged heresy. It is clear that she knows considerably more of God than her examiners, both the conservatives and the liberals. As Maitland sees her out, he feels the desperate need to ask her a simple and unforgivable question.

> 'Sister Martin,' Maitland called after her from the door, 'I haven't time to stand on ceremony. Have you—' He lost his temper at his powers of speech and ended in saying lamely, 'Have you *seen* God?'
>
> . . . She smiled. 'If I said yes, father, I could hardly blame you for calling me a liar . . . What would you expect to be told, father? That you see God as you see a town clerk, at a given time on a given day? And as if by appointment?'
>
> . . . Costello coughed a summons to him. The nun formed a sudden resolve. She told him, 'One knows by the results. Nothing is the same afterwards. Everything has a special . . . luminosity. You are able to see, well, *existence* shining in things.' She shrugged, 'Words again!' and seemed very sad.[6]

To receive the truth as it is in Christ is to find oneself at home in this way in the world, seeing 'existence shining in things', seeing the world as expressing the self-gift of God. When the hospitality of God's being is seen through the complex inter-relation of Jesus, the God to whom he prays and the Spirit whose coming he promises, we are not only welcomed, we are

6 Thomas Keneally, *Three Cheers for the Paraclete*, London: Penguin, 1968, pp. 158–9.

also set free to offer welcome: welcome in our vision and understanding of the whole material order, welcome to one another. Our place in the world is not the territory for which we must fight, but a home into which the world, the other, can be invited. Hence, of course, the fear this can inspire, both in us and others: perhaps we shrink from receiving fully the loving gift of God because we sense that it will make us images and bearers of God's hospitality – and if we look at Jesus on trial, Jesus crucified, we know the cost of that.

On trial with Christ

All the trial narratives of the Gospels come to place one single charge against us: we choose to be somewhere other than where Christ is. Each Gospel in its own way challenges us to step down from the tribunal to stand with him. For Mark, we must stand in the lonely moment of 'useless' witness. For Matthew, we must distance ourselves from the expertise and the religiosity that make us strangers to God's surprises. For Luke, we must find a voice for and with those who are locked out. Finally, in the face of John's narrative, we must decide not simply which 'kingdom' we belong to, but which *world* we are going to live in: the world that is made sense of by the vision of the creator's self-gift or the world that defines itself against its maker and so breeds refusal and rivalry in all its dealings.

In each Gospel, what focuses and grounds the challenge is that the trial brings to light not so much a set of facts about Jesus but the truth of his *identity* – as the one who is entitled to say 'I am'; as the embodiment of God's Wisdom; as the centre of a moral world at odds with the world with which we are familiar; as the place where truth is. Faith in Jesus is not bound first to the establishing of facts about him – remember how briskly this is disposed of by John in his account of the trial before Annas. Concern with such facts is and must always be related to who he is and what must be said about his identity as a whole. However much we know about Jesus, the verdict on who he is can only be delivered if we are willing to move, willing to be on trial both with him and before him. We cannot properly say who he is unless we have stood before his tribunal and discovered from him something of who *we* are.

The decision we face

This is not the place to delve into the convoluted question of the relation between the Jesus of history and the Christ of faith, nor do I wish to suggest that the details of Jesus' life are irrelevant to faith, but it is nonetheless important to see why the evangelists give so much emphasis to their trial stories. The point is that here, as we see Jesus standing before the tribunal, we have to decide what our own response will be. Without this, and without the execution that follows, we could just about get away with seeing belief in Christ as obedience to his teaching and conviction on the basis of his miracles. Faith is neither of these, however, because *it requires us to move from our centre to his* – and this is what the trial stories seek to help us achieve.

We have seen already what the cost is. If the place of Jesus were a place that could be mapped onto the world as we know it and with which we are comfortable, it would merely stand alongside all the other places and systems. So much we have said. It is not a place that can be mapped in such a way. However, if it is a place that is everywhere and nowhere, not confined yet not competing, it will menace the conflicts and competitions of the world. As we move on now to look at the history of Jesus' community, we shall discover how that cost was and is understood and experienced.

Questions for reflection and discussion

1 What sort of things do you associate with calling Jesus 'king'?

2 Can you think of some ways in which Christians try to defend or protect Jesus? What risks do you see in such efforts?

3 Where have you found healing in the Church's life – for yourself or for anyone else?

4 Should Christians be 'unworldly'? If so, in what sense?

5 What do we really want from the Church in our lives?

Prayer

Jesus,
make us tell the truth about ourselves;
help us not to be afraid of meeting you
and seeing ourselves with your eyes.
Help us to care more about the truth and love we see in you
than about anything the world may say or do.
Amen.

CHAPTER FIVE

God's Spies: Believers on Trial

Stories of the martyrs

The Christian faith gave to the world two quite distinctive and new forms of literature: the Gospel and the detached 'passion story' of the Christian martyrs. Throughout the second Christian century, churches around the Mediterranean exchanged, developed and refined the records of the trials and executions of their members. One of the main items of currency in relations between churches was the martyr story. It was as if the churches competed with one another to produce these witnesses of integrity, and also sought to give each other a share in their achievements.

Telling a story of persecution and death to another Christian community is telling that community about God's faithfulness in the life of the Church, and about the tangible power of God which produces these victories over fear and hatred. A death endured in Christlike patience shows that the death of Jesus truly changes what can happen in the human world. The exchange of these stories between communities reinforces the unity of the faith across the Roman Empire: what is done and suffered here echoes what is done and suffered there. If the same faith is held in different settings, the same consequences can be expected. If the same sufferings are experienced, this in turn confirms the sameness of the faith. These themes are already around in the New Testament (notably in Hebrews and 1 Peter), but it is as the second century unfolds that the martyr records come fully into their own as a means of strengthening the Church's unity, and indeed as a means of theological reflection.

Standing their ground

In some ways the most poignant narratives are those which dryly record the bare details of a trial and the fact of an execution. In AD 180, 12 North African Christians were examined at Carthage by the proconsul Saturninus. Their names suggest that they were slaves, of native background. The account of their trial gives only the barest details – no drama, no miracles, not even a description of their deaths; simply the dialogue between the proconsul and Speratus, evidently the leader of the little group.[1] The proconsul is civilized and humane: there is no problem about securing the indulgence of the Emperor if the accused will pull themselves together and go through the motions of civic piety, taking an oath by the *genius*, the divine power, of the Emperor. He gently explains to Speratus that he, the proconsul, and other good citizens are pious people too, and their *religio* is as simple as could be; all that is needed to count as a good and religious person is the

---

1 'The Passion of the Scillitan Martyrs' is translated in J. Stevenson (ed.), *A New Eusebius: Documents Illustrative of the History of the Church to AD 337*, London: SPCK, 1957 (and many later editions), no. 22. See also Herbert Musurillo (ed.), *The Acts of the Christian Martyrs*, Oxford: Clarendon Press, 1972.

oath by the Emperor's *genius* and prayer for his wellbeing. What can conceivably be the problem?

You can hear in the dialogue the patience of the educated man trying to make things easy for the uneducated: look, this is easy; look, we are really concerned about the same things. Do you want an adjournment to think about it? Up to 30 days? Don't be silly, it can all be very simple and painless, and no one will think any the worse of you. The replies come back, from Speratus and the others: they have committed no crime; they pay taxes; they pray for the Emperor's wellbeing – but what they do, they do because of a commandment from a source other than the government. They are Christians. When they are offered a chance to take a month to think about it, they simply repeat that statement: we are Christians. There is nothing more to be said, nothing more to reflect on; their social loyalty is anchored somewhere else. So the end comes: 'Saturninus the proconsul read out the sentence from his tablet: Speratus, Nartzalus, Cittinus, Donata, Vestia, Secunda and the rest have admitted that they live according to the usage of the Christians. Since they have obstinately persevered even when offered the chance of returning to Roman custom, the sentence is that they should be beheaded.'

Sacred and secular identities

This stark little document is heavily charged with theological concerns. Speratus may not be – at least by the proconsul's standards – an educated man, but he identifies with uncanny accuracy just where the heart of the difficulty lies. Christians are good members of society in completely *secular* terms: they keep the law and pray for good order, but they do not see their obedience to the law as based on any conviction about the sacredness of the legal system or the lawgiver. They observe the prosaic duties of society for reasons quite unconnected with the society itself. When pressed, Speratus is explicit in saying that Christians have nothing to do with the *imperium* of this world, since they serve a God 'whom no one has ever seen or can see with human eyes'.

This explains the strange fact that Christians were called 'atheists' by their Roman neighbours. They denied that the gods were simply *there* to be seen and dealt with in and through the things of the world and the political realities of the world. In a rather paradoxical way, they based their faith on the absence of God – God's absence from the powers and conventions that organized their society. The invisible and transcendent God they worshipped laid obligations on them that had everything to do with how they lived in society. That is why Speratus can protest that he and his companions are dependable participants in social life, strangers to malice, gossip and selfishness, willing to share responsibility for the public sphere (i.e., they pay their taxes). Obedience to God comes first, however, and this is entirely different from obedience to any given structure of power. It is a perspective that anticipates the sort of thing the Reformers were to say so many centuries later (especially Luther and Tyndale): the Christian acts righteously and serves the social good because of the indwelling of God's gracious gift, which overflows in giving – not because good or generous social behaviour is the currency in which you pay to secure your welfare in time or in eternity.

Martyrdom only begins to make sense if you believe in an 'invisible' God, because it takes for granted that Christian actions are not directed at any visible reward. We are pointed back to Mark's Gospel again, to the 'uselessness' of faith and stability. The accounts of the martyr trials make much of the sense – very clear in the North African case quoted above – of simply not being *able* to act otherwise, not being able to deny what one is. Old Bishop Polycarp, facing the magistrate and the mob in the arena at Smyrna in AD 156, replies to the invitation to swear by the Emperor's divinity with the famous words, 'Eighty-six years have I served him, and he has done me no harm. How can I blaspheme my king who has saved me?' When the invitation is repeated, he continues by accusing the magistrate of pretending not to know who he, Polycarp, is: he is a Christian.[2] Who he *is* decides what he will and will not do, what he can and cannot do; and he is the subject of another king, the receiver of a gift of free salvation. We noted how the trial stories of the Gospels were not ultimately about what Jesus did or said but about who he was. The same holds true in the martyr narratives. The issue is who the believer is, and whether or not this is a person whose life is defined by the sovereignty of God's free gift.

Power and obedience

The martyr stories, therefore, are also about where *power* is recognized, and what kind of power. Polycarp's allegiance to Jesus as king is rooted in his confidence that Jesus has saved him, that Jesus has made him the gift of his (Polycarp's) life. The power that counts for the martyr is a power that bestows

2 Polycarp's martyrdom is recorded in Stevenson, *A New Eusebius*, no. 18. See also Musurillo, *The Acts of the Christian Martyrs*.

life, not a power that simply commands. God's will can be done, and the martyr can maintain loyalty to Jesus under the most appalling threats, because something has been imparted (not ordered) – a new depth of truthful living, a new and deeper centre to the self relocated in the life of Jesus, or standing in the place where Jesus stands.

Power that sets out to command or control is at best secondary to this, and cannot be recognized as having any right to overturn the power of Jesus' kingship. That is why the martyrs were so important in the Early Church: they demonstrated very plainly where the centre of Christian life lay and what it meant to obey Christ as ruler. Obedience comes as a result of what is given; it is the search to find adequate ways of showing gratitude, allowing the gift to pervade and fill the whole of a human identity. The martyr's trial is a deeply political contest, opposing two incompatible kinds of power and two incompatible kinds of obedience. The believer is the one who rejects an obedience based on the sacredness of the way things are in the world, in favour of an obedience that arises irresistibly from the sense of something new bestowed or shared.

Political contests

Yet precisely because martyrdom is political in this way, because it has to do with fundamental questions about the identity of Christians, the telling of martyr stories can easily slip back into the ordinary sort of political contest – between two sorts of *comparable* power, fighting for the same territory. We can already see a shadow of this in the letters of Polycarp's friend Ignatius, in the early years of the second century, on his way to execution in Rome. He is about to suffer an agonizing death for his faith, and because of this he can appeal to his forthcoming agony in order to reinforce the weight of what he says to the churches to whom he is writing. Martyrdom gives authority.

In the middle of the third century, the Church in North Africa was bitterly divided over who had the right to readmit sinners to communion. Some of those who had been imprisoned and tortured during persecutions claimed that their authority outweighed that of the local church through its bishop, since they had suffered for their faith and so had acquired spiritual power. Those who gave their allegiance to the sufferers were all too ready to despise the rest as cowards and traitors, polluting the Church's purity. More and more divisions arose in the Church over just this point: in the first 350 years of the Church's life, it was not doctrinal disputes that created the bitterest and most long-lasting schisms, but quarrels provoked by attitudes to martyrs and martyrdom. In the twentieth century, there is plenty of evidence for similar tensions in countries where persecution has been heavy. A study of the Russian Orthodox Church since 1917, for example, would reveal many of these issues to be still alive and well, albeit in rather different forms.

Misuse of martyrdom

Even more troubling, though, is the way in which martyr stories begin to breed fantasies of revenge. Early in the fourth century the Christian historian Lactantius wrote a substantial chronicle dealing with the deaths of those who had persecuted the Church, designed to show that God unfailingly avenged his saints by arranging horrible fates for their judges. It is a style of thinking that is clearly foreshadowed in some pages of the New Testament itself; it becomes part of the emotional energy behind the worst kinds of Christian anti-Semitism; it is, in short, an attempt to unlearn all that the trial stories of the Gospels are meant to teach. The hidden hand of God, the transcendence of God that refuses to compete with worldly power, is shown to be no more than a temporary arrangement. God will, fairly soon, step in to show that he is just as capable of violent success as any earthly authority. His kingdom *is* of this world after all.

Christians sometimes seem to show a kind of relief when this is said. Yes, of course Jesus accepted his death and refused defence and revenge – but that was yesterday. It was necessary that he should die for our salvation, but once that death is over and done with, the patterns of power can return as they were, only this time administered by the right people. Yes, of course God is merciful for now, and you still have a chance of repentance – but quite soon he will exercise his justice and the universe will be tidy once again. Yes, of course the blood of the martyrs is the seed of the Church, and the brave and selfless suffering of believers is an example to us – but it is also a wonderful support to our cause that people have died for it, and we must be careful to maintain complete loyalty and purity so as not to dishonour their glorious memory. And so on. The use – the exploitation – of stories of suffering is a major element in the way Christians have organized and defended their life together, and it is another area in which Jesus' trial summons us to trial too.

Honesty versus exploitation

Bishop Lancelot Andrewes, preaching before the king on Whitsunday in 1615, is scathing about how some Christians are not content with the nonviolence of the primitive Church. Have we not grown out of this early idealism? Now we must have 'Christians of a new edition', marked not by the sign of the Holy Spirit as the dove descending but by some more aggressive symbol:

> They were to be so [peaceful] but for a time, till their beaks and talons were grown, till their strength was come to them, and they able to make their party good; and then this dove here might take her wings, fly whither she would, 'and take her ease'; then a new Holy Ghost to come down upon them that would not take it as the other did, but take arms, depose, deprive, blow up; instead of an olive-branch, have a match-light in her beak or a bloody knife.[3]

We shall have to have a new Holy Spirit – and so a new baptism and a new Christ, or else 'make a strange metamorphosis of the old; clap him on a crooked beak, and stick him full of eagle's feathers, and force him to do contrary to that He was wont, and to that His nature is'.[4] In truth, however, the Spirit is not changeable, and the characteristics he bestows on the Church are what they always were. To turn the Spirit into

3 Lancelot Andrewes, *Ninety-Six Sermons*, Volume III, Oxford and London: James Parker, 1875, p. 259.
4 Ibid.

the consuming fire of violence is to deny the essential and unchanging nature of God's work.

It is a fine and witty passage, but when we have read it, it is worth remembering that Andrewes intends it as an attack on contemporary Roman Catholics because of their apparent espousing of violent terrorism in the Gunpowder Plot. Elsewhere he recommends with relish the hanging, drawing and quartering of Catholic conspirators and 'Jesuits' (something of a blanket term at the time for treasonous Catholic clergy). His words ironically illustrate just the traps we have been considering.

There is such a fine line, it seems, between martyrdom as the acknowledgement and demonstration of a different kind of power and martyrdom as a bid for the same power, something that will be a trump card in the struggle for control of the world. It serves to remind us of the fine line in all our experience between coming to terms honestly with what we have suffered and using our suffering as a weapon, a justification, an alibi. It is hard to be both truthful about our pain and careful about the temptation to cling to the position of victim. Nonetheless, that is the challenge: to understand that what is revealed in the martyr's trial is also what is revealed in the trial of Jesus – the simple difference between God and the way the world organizes itself.

The challenge of different environments

Perhaps, in our own suspicious and complicated age, these stories of drama and cost are harder for us to respond to unselfconsciously. We may feel that the records of the Early Church are wonderful testimonies to the youthful simplicity of belief: 'Speratus said for the second time, "I am a Christian"; and all the others said the same.'[5] It is not just a historical problem. In the mid-eighties, my wife and I spent a few months in Southern Africa, working for the Anglican Church there. We returned, I remember, conscious of the human complexity of so many of the situations we had seen and shared; not (I hope) too romantic about the heroism of the South African Church, but still overwhelmed by a kind of nostalgia for a situation where at least the choices seemed more dramatically clear. There really was a sense in which you had to answer certain central questions about where you stood and with whom you belonged.

Returning to Britain meant returning to a context with far less clarity about these central questions, a context in which it was harder to know what sort of 'resistance' was either possible or constructive. As we told stories of what we had experienced or heard, we were aware that it was no easy task to translate what we had learned into this apparently more confused and weary environment. Our experience, of course, was only a pale reflection of what many of the great figures of the South African struggle felt after they had been deported or forced out. The recent biography of Trevor Huddleston asks, in effect, whether anywhere could have been a real home to him after the years of draining, exhilarating and fantastically risky work in Sophiatown in the forties and fifties.[6] Other settings must so often have felt trivial and colourless, a different moral world under a grey and cloudy sky.

5 'The Passion of the Scillitan Martyrs', op. cit.
6 See Robin Denniston, *Trevor Huddleston: A Life*, London: Macmillan, 1999.

It is possible to look at the Early Church just as we are inclined to look at South Africa, Russia, Nazi Germany or any other of the great sites of witness in our age. In our own relatively stable environment, we will feel that we have missed the excitement, that we can never be Christians like *that*. Something of this sense must also have been around in the century or so after Christianity had become a legal religion in the Roman Empire, when serious believers took to the deserts and the mountains to live the monastic life. Nothing else was now going to be for them the kind of testing that once was required of Christians in the face of the state's violence. Monasticism (and later, in the Celtic world, voluntary exile from the homeland) was spoken of as a contemporary equivalent of martyrdom.

We can trivialize this, I suppose: since no one else is going to make me suffer, I shall have to do it for myself. Yet it is remarkable how alert the early monastic writers often are to this twist of motivation, how often they remind the would-be ascetic that the real test is stability in the repetitive, dry pattern of life that inevitably develops in monastic communities. It is also noticeable how the language of test and trial receives its most detailed elaboration in monastic literature. The urge to go somewhere else and do something more obviously worthwhile; the intense frustration of prayer, day in and day out, without clear experiences of joy and love; the need to live alongside diverse and often annoying people without yielding constantly to the longing to put them right or to score over them – this is the realm of monastic 'trial', chronicled in remorseless detail (and not without some ironic humour) by the monastic fathers and mothers. It may be that these wry celebrations of the prose of Christian heroism have rather a lot to say to us when we yearn after the dramas of martyrdom.

Finding freedom in everyday life

What is martyrdom about? Essentially, it is about something other than heroism. It has to do with freedom from the imperatives of violence – a freedom, in this instance, that carries the most dramatic cost imaginable. It is not the drama that matters, however, it is the freedom that is important. If we focus on the drama, if we long for the opportunity of heroism, we are in thrall to another kind of violence because we are seeking a secure and morally impregnable place for the self to be. We want to be victims, to enter a world where there are clear divisions between the forces of darkness and the forces of light. We want, in fact, to get back to that clear frontier between insiders and outsiders which is so comprehensively unsettled by the trial of Jesus in the Gospels. What we have to ask is how this freedom is to be realized when the test, the trial, is the undramatic context of daily life – or, to go back to the language of earlier chapters, how a life which may never have to face violent challenge may yet express the *truth* that violence is overcome and silenced in Christ.

There is no brief and general answer. We can make a start at identifying the problems, finding our own equivalents to the monastic temptations listed above, but the central issue is actually very much the same as the question we examined in the last chapter: what it means to be at home in the world. We come back to this paradox repeatedly – that when we are most radically at odds with how the world runs itself, we are most fully at home in creation, growing in the habit of receiving reality as a gift. What this reflection on martyrdom brings into focus for us is that a concern with the drama of our lives is one of the things that most significantly gets in the way of such being at home.

When I dramatize my situation, seeking for a role that will best display my own account of my virtues, courage or wisdom, setting up a conflict (a trial?) that will draw a clear line between my stance and that of the feared or despised other, I refuse the hospitality of truth. To overcome the pull towards drama, I have to practise seeing the situation through other eyes, 'de-centring' myself as best I can and deliberately putting in question my own stance. I shall do this most effectively by a mixture of imagination and conversation (remember Elizabeth Templeton's 'conversation towards truth'). I have to face, and face down, my boredom, my expectation that the world will always give me satisfying roles to play. To put it more positively, I have to make an art of ordinary living.

Fear of freedom

To 'take upon 's the mystery of things / As if we were God's spies' is the aspiration of King Lear as he and Cordelia are hustled off to prison.[7] They will nurture in their cells, he says, a perception of how the world is that is free from intrigue and ambition; they will see the truth, living in repeated reconciliation with each other. 'We'll live, / And pray, and sing, and tell old tales, and laugh / At gilded butterflies.'[8] It is a poignant picture of undramatic life, and it will instantly be broken by

7 William Shakespeare, *King Lear*, Act 5, scene 3, ll. 16–17.
8 Ibid., ll. 11–13.

the renewed violence of Lear's enemies, killing Cordelia and breaking his heart. Nonetheless, it is a 'transparent' moment amidst the horror and vengefulness of the play. It is, simply, *possible* to see freely, not to be caught up in the pathetic struggle for honour and precedence.

The world is none too happy with the presence of spies from another order, however, and the peaceful existence of which Lear dreams is not to be his. As surely as the martyrs of the Early Church, he has to die because he will not be a citizen on the terms dictated by the powers of the world. He sees something else, and this is frightening for the powers of the world which long so fiercely to control what can be seen. Anita Mason's *The Illusionist* again gives us a sharp insight, as the condemned slave Demetrius faces his judge:

> **The trial was taking place somewhere else. From an immeasurable distance, he was aware of the governor's face staring at him in a passion of fury. Demetrius looked at the face and saw that this man too would one day die. He looked deep into the furious eyes, and far away at the back of them he saw fear.[9]**

Fear is not meant to be seen in the powerful. Should we read the desperate insistence of Roman magistrates that it was still possible for the accused to change their minds as a sign of fear – fear that in the eyes of their victims they were being seen as mortal and fragile, as people standing under the judgement of a power they could not begin to comprehend or control?

9 Mason, *The Illusionist*, p. 227.

If, on the other hand, we turn again to the Gospels, we are reminded how frequent is the command, 'Do not be afraid.' To live in the truth is to experience freedom from fear. To the extent that our daily life is conditioned by fear (of failure, of others, of too much of the same, of too much change, of death, of our own desires and our own weaknesses), it is indeed in this 'theatre' that we have to display the sovereignty of the power that gives life to us. Making an art of our daily life is really about living without fear; doing what we do not out of anxiety that if something is *not* done our whole reality will collapse or deliver us into the hands of someone or something else, but out of the inner pressure to 'incarnate' what has been given to us, to give it flesh, voice and locality.

The art of daily life

Art always has about it the dimension of freedom. It is not there to do a job or prop things up; it exists, most artists would say, because some form, some vision presses itself upon us, in ways we cannot fully perceive in advance. So if we talk about 'the art of daily life', we are evoking this strange freedom – not a freedom to make things up from nothing, to do and say whatever we please, but a freedom from the need to meet obligations all the time, a freedom (in the case of the believer's life) to give to human actions a shape and meaning rooted in what has been given to us.

There are so many ways of expressing this – the Jewish saying that the patriarch Enoch was a cobbler, and with every stitch joining the upper and lower leather of the shoe he reunited the glory above with the glory below; the Russian Orthodox habit of describing the daily 'housekeeping' observances of monastic

life as 'obediences', acts of concrete surrender to the gift of God;
the Lutheran conviction that domestic, commercial, labouring
and political life were all 'vocations'. In each of these visions,
there is at the centre a displacement of the busy and frantic ego,
trying to impose an individual will on the world. That displacement is freedom. It is an alarming freedom and a costly
one, and it is intimately related to the freedom of the martyr,
whose 'displacement' is the most costly of all.

Martyrdom is the ultimate statement of belonging in and
to the world as God made it, not to a particular order of
earthly authority. This is a paradoxical way of putting it,
because martyrdom can so easily be seen as the ultimate
statement of indifference to or rejection of the world. Yet, if
our reading of John's Gospel in the previous chapter was at
all correct, the implication of living in the truth of Jesus is
that it means being at home in the world, and this is what
threatens the world's systems of power, because it gives no
legitimacy to the defensive violence and fear of the other that
mark these systems. When there are questions to be raised
about a particular martyr story or about its use by Christians,
they will be questions about what lies behind the act of costly witness: is it this matter of being at home in the world, or
is it a passion to deny creation for the sake of God alone?

Questionable martyrs

Such questions do arise, and have done so from the beginning of Christianity to our own day. There are deaths that
cannot be called anything other than heroic, but that uncomfortably suggest just such an impatience with creation. Their
affinity is not with the sacramental vision of everyday life, but

rather with the violence of extreme asceticism. Augustine and others describe the groups of dissidents who wandered North Africa in the late fourth century, begging for martyrdom and threatening violence if they were not killed – perhaps the most bizarre expression of this quirk of Christian motivation. There are also less dramatic instances, and even some of the best-known martyr stories across the centuries may make us wonder at times. Ignatius of Antioch's almost manic eagerness to get to the arena is certainly near the borderline. Oddly enough, the businesslike intervention of Perpetua, helping her nervous executioner to strike in the right place – 'Oh, let *me* do that, for goodness' sake!' – somehow seems rather less problematic.[10]

This may explain why modern readers are so often struck by stories of unlikely and reluctant martyrs, the antiheroes of this literature. The martyrs of the Reformation era, on both sides, sometimes touch us precisely because of their flaws and evasions. Thomas More and Thomas Cranmer are figures of unceasing fascination, partly because each would certainly have thought the execution of the other to be a good thing. Both were implicated as fully as could be in a profoundly violent state system, although Cranmer has a somewhat better record in trying to intervene for the king's victims. Both sought to use all their exceptional intelligence in order to avoid execution. Both recognized (although Cranmer did not see it until the very end) that they had been brought to a place where there were no more choices to be made. Those moments of clarity and freedom do not and cannot excuse

10 'The Passion of Perpetua and Felicity' is included in Musurillo, *The Acts of the Christian Martyrs.*

their earlier record, but they do tell us that somehow the perception of a world under God had remained alive in them, deeply enough to enable them to meet their deaths as they did. Neither of them received their sentences or went to their deaths cursing their enemies – More even expressed a disarming prayer that he and his judges would 'meet merrily in heaven'.

There is a kind of reassurance in this. If we looked at More during his period of office as Lord Chancellor, or Cranmer in the last years of King Henry's reign, we would probably think that they were not unattractive figures, less obnoxious, certainly, than many of their contemporaries, but still essentially locked into a framework so alien and repellent that we should not easily imagine them as capable of challenging or inspiring a later generation. Nor should we immediately guess that they would die exemplary deaths: they were neither of them cowards, but both, at the peak of their careers, shared just the same servility towards the monarch as everyone else in court circles. Both were aware – although More expressed it more clearly – that the king's favour could vanish overnight, that they were in thrall to an arbitrary and almost insane despotism, but both continued to serve this tyranny.[11]

How it was that both discovered at the end not only the freedom to die but – at least in More's case – even a kind of ironic detachment about it is bound to be mysterious, but it

11 Thomas More's son-in-law, William Roper, famously reported a conversation between More and the Duke of Norfolk, in which Norfolk warned More that 'it is perilous striving with Princes . . . for, by God's body, Master More, *indignatio principis mors est* [the anger of the prince is death]'. More replied, 'Is that all, my Lord? . . . Then in good faith is there no more difference between your Grace and me, but that I shall die today and you tomorrow' (William Roper and Nicholas Harpsfield, *Lives of Saint Thomas More*, E.E. Reynolds (ed.), London: Dent, 1963, p. 35).

does say to us that God's freedom may be growing secretly in all sorts of unlikely people. We may not have a chance to see it if the great hour of public trial never comes, but it is still there nevertheless. It may even be there in us, who shrink at the idea of suffering for our faith or anything else. This is where it helps to be undramatic. If we felt sure of our willingness and ability to make unimaginable sacrifices in the future, if we were able to imagine without shame and terror how we would react if we were faced with persecution, we should have succeeded in taking possession of our future and enthroning our favoured image of ourselves. We do not and cannot know the future, however. What we therefore have to do is what, presumably, More and Cranmer did in the midst of their compromised and murky lives: we have to make room for God in prayer and repentance, *day after day*. At the time of trial it will become apparent how honest we have been in inviting God in. Meanwhile, there is only the daily art of faith, the necessary prose of Christian speech.

Facing up to the cost

This should not be read as a recommendation to get on with domestic things and ask no questions about our public life. In this respect, at least, we are bound to part company with the sixteenth-century mind. Gradually, in the Western world, power has become more accountable and it is therefore all the more important to be able to ask about the human cost of public decisions. To stand with the martyrs in the truth, to accept our commission as 'God's spies', means that we have not only the freedom but also the obligation to attempt to see through certain kinds of social and political evasiveness. It has been said often enough that our society is bad at 'mourning'. We do not like to be reminded about loss and fragility (which may be why there are sometimes such disproportionate expressions of grief and desolation about events that do not touch us all that directly, such as the death of Diana, Princess of Wales).

In the late nineties, Britain and other countries took up arms against tyrannical regimes elsewhere in the world. These military adventures may or may not have been justified or helpful, but the underlying problem for the Christian is how to be truthful about them. Yes, there is a cost in civilian deaths. Yes, such and such a policy, at home or abroad, will cost resources that will not therefore be available for other things. Yes, politics is frequently about choosing where the cost will come, not about finding a cost-free option. The Christian is certainly called on to take up the unpopular position of being the person who asks about specific costs, about the *tragic* element in public decisions – not to turn the screws of guilt, but to remind us that facing cost is the only adult way of understanding the full nature of freedom. The Christian may also be the person who has the still more unpopular task of saying that *this* particular cost is unacceptable in terms of social or international wellbeing or public integrity.

Such awkwardness comes, I would suggest, not from the conviction that we occupy a higher moral plane, but simply from the sense that we have to say what it has been given us to see, even when (as is all too usual) we possess little clarity about how to make a better job of it. We can at least ask that we behave as and are treated as adults, capable of acknowledging the price we pay for our actions. Believers, shaped by the stories of the trials of their Lord and his witnesses, will know that the price of untruth is the highest price of all, for a person or a society. The same applies to a Church, of course: when a Christian community refuses to face its own failures or tragedies, refuses to mourn, it moves away from being at home in the world through living in the truth.

The descent into untruth may come from the refusal to face the realities of a pastoral failure (I am writing as a bishop unhappily aware of how many such failures I shall have to confess), the refusal to deal honestly with a traumatic situation such as child abuse in a parish, the refusal to accept that a decision will really hurt or that a decision has really been made, the refusal to admit waning influence or confusion over some matter of policy . . . I could go on, but the problem is clear enough. Real life in Christ requires us to look death in the face – the little deaths of dishonesty and evasion as much as the great risks faith may run. In the final chapter, we shall be turning to some modern reflections on the cost of escape, considering how much we have to pay – or lose – if we run away from the tribunal.

Questions for reflection and discussion

1 Why were the early Christians called 'atheists'?

2 How important for a Christian is loyalty to the nation or the state?

3 Do you think you have ever used your own suffering to obtain an advantage over someone else?

4 Does it make sense to think of your daily life as a 'sacrament'?

5 If you look at the life of a martyr from another Christian tradition – or even another faith – does it help you to understand their beliefs better?

Prayer

Jesus,
save us from making great dramas of our lives,
help us grow up,
help us make sense of the daily routine,
so that we are rooted deeply enough in you
to face the hardest crises when they come.
Amen.

CHAPTER SIX

No Answer: Jesus and his Judges

The Grand Inquisitor

Without doubt, the best known trial of Jesus in modern literature remains the chapter in Dostoyevsky's *The Brothers Karamazov* entitled 'The Grand Inquisitor'. It has become almost a cliché for literary-minded expositors of the Christian faith, but it keeps its power to shock and disturb in a remarkable way – not least because it leaves us with a resolution in the form of a single powerful image, the kind of thing that may make all the difference or none at all. It is the climax of the argument in Book 5 of the novel between the radical Ivan and his younger brother Alyosha, a monastic novice – an argument not so much about whether God exists as about whether belief in God is morally defensible.

In the preceding chapter, Ivan's catalogue of innocent suffering, specifically the sufferings of abused and tortured children, is probably the most eloquent attack on easy theories of divine justice or divine reparation ever written by a Christian.[1]

---

1 Fyodor Dostoyevsky, *The Brothers Karamazov*, trans. David Magarshack, London: Penguin Classics, 1958, Book 5, Chapter 4 'Rebellion', Volume 1, pp. 276–88.

At the end of this chapter, Ivan asks his brother whether he could imagine guaranteeing the welfare and stability of the universe at the cost of torturing to death one little girl – 'to found the edifice on her unavenged tears' – and Alyosha replies, 'softly', that he would be unable to do this. But, says Ivan, does faith not require that we must believe exactly this, that we accept our salvation at the price of unspeakable, gratuitous suffering? Alyosha protests: the edifice is founded not on the terrible contingency of particular outrages but on the one who gives his own innocent blood for the sake of the world.[2] Ivan's response is the story of the Inquisitor.

Appealing to Jesus as a way out of the unbearable contemplation of the pain of others is, for Ivan, a strategy that fails to engage with what Jesus really is. The Inquisitor chapter continues the prosecution of God, this time using the unique figure who gives his name to the story as an accusing angel. Readers at the time, and many interpreters from Orthodox and Protestant backgrounds, assumed and have continued to assume that the novelist's target is totalitarian religion, that the chapter is primarily a kind of satire on ideological tyranny. While he is not averse to some facile sneers at Catholicism, however, Dostoyevsky is a good deal more subtle than that, and we have to read this story honestly, as a 'thought experiment' pushing as far as it can in pressing a case against Christ.

The case against Jesus

The stage setting is conventional (as many have pointed out, bits of it owe a heavy debt to Verdi's opera *Don Carlos*); Christ

2 Ibid., pp. 287–8.

returns to earth at the time of the Inquisition in sixteenth-century Spain, performs miracles, raises the dead, and is arrested at the Grand Inquisitor's command. At night, the Inquisitor visits his prisoner's cell. 'He approaches him slowly, puts the lamp on the table and says to him: "Is it you? You?"'[3] What follows is far from conventional. The Inquisitor goes over the temptations of Jesus in the desert, arguing that his refusal of 'miracle, mystery and authority' have made him the enemy of real, tangible human happiness. Jesus overestimates what humanity is capable of; he speaks only to the strong, not the weak (a striking reversal of what is often said).

The Inquisitor and his allies, in Church and state, will guarantee the happiness Jesus cannot give, even at the price of lying to the masses. They take on themselves the guilt of deceit because people cannot bear the burden of freedom. 'Why,' asks the Inquisitor, 'is the weak soul to blame for being unable to receive gifts so terrible? Surely, you did not come only to the chosen and for the chosen?'[4] Humanity at large will become happy and guilt-free children; the rulers of humanity suffer in silence. The Inquisitor himself has been fasting in the wilderness. 'I, too, blessed freedom, with which you have blessed men, and . . . I, too, was preparing to stand among your chosen ones, among the strong and mighty . . . But I woke up and refused to serve madness . . . I went away from the proud and returned to the meek for the happiness of the meek'.[5]

Perhaps, Ivan speculates, spurred by Alyosha's baffled protests, the Catholic Church has been run for centuries by a

---

3 Ibid., p. 293.
4 Ibid., p. 301.
5 Ibid., p. 305.

secret fellowship of such compassionate atheists, spiritual rulers who love humanity more than God does because they will not insist upon a response of free love. He defends the Inquisitor against his brother's conventional religious condemnation, because he understands that the Inquisitor is both morally serious and deeply tragic: he surrenders truth for the sake of love. Plato, in his account of the vocation of the rulers in his work *The Republic*, had long before sketched the paradox of the person who sees the truth and then has to step back from it in order to govern the world in accordance with it, even if this means that his own happiness must be sacrificed. He guarantees justice for all, sees that all have what they need, but has to be unjust to himself, never having his own heart's desire. Dostoyevsky turns the screw a little more by insisting that the ruler in this parable must actively *deny* the truth to his subjects, because truth and happiness cannot live together.

Negative vision

The Inquisitor is a wise man, and he describes the devil of Jesus' temptations as a 'terrible and wise spirit, the spirit of self-destruction and nonexistence'.[6] It is a disturbing bringing together of what seem opposites. How can wisdom be so connected to nonexistence? What does it mean to say, as Ivan does, that this spirit presents another kind of truth, a truth that Jesus will not confront? Ivan's Inquisitor implies that the truth of the human condition is bleak: most people are not capable of love without reassurance; all will die; most will suffer. Beneath the surface the pattern is indeed self-destruction and

6 Ibid., p. 295.

nonexistence. What is needed, therefore, is not the appeal to a barely possible freedom, but order and controlled distraction from the truth. Who could be brave enough for disinterested love in such a climate? The requirement to love and believe without miracle and problem-solving can only spell despair.

Or perhaps, faced with the 'wisdom' of this negative vision, people will opt for manifestly self-destructive behaviour. William Golding's *Darkness Visible* evokes just the impact of this vision in a small girl, Sophy, who is to grow into the pivotal point of destructiveness in the book. 'She had been told it often enough but now she *saw* it. You could choose to belong to people . . . Or you could choose what was real and what you knew was real – your own self sitting inside with its own wishes and rules at the mouth of the tunnel.'[7] Dostoyevsky's Ivan is challenged by Alyosha as to whether he is going to join the select band of workers for human illusion and happiness, but he replies by repeating his earlier aphorism that 'all is permitted'. He will burn himself out by the time he is 30, because he has seen (so he believes) the truth and has no desire to conceal it from himself or from others.

The ending of this trial scene is probably its most famous moment. The Inquisitor waits for a response. 'The old man would have liked him to say something, however bitter and terrible. But he suddenly approached the old man and kissed him gently on his bloodless, aged lips.' The Inquisitor flings open the door and tells his prisoner to go and never return.[8] What happens to him? asks Alyosha, and Ivan replies, 'The kiss glows in his heart, but the old man sticks to his ideas.'[9] When

7 William Golding, *Darkness Visible*, London: Faber, 1979, p. 123.
8 Dostoyevsky, *The Brothers Karamazov*, p. 308.
9 Ibid.

Ivan, at the end of his final outburst, concludes by saying that
Alyosha is bound to repudiate him, his younger brother
echoes the prisoner in the story and wordlessly kisses him.

Choosing a response

It is a far more complex story than it seems at first, because it is
not about tyranny and freedom but about truth and falsehood,
about what humanity is actually like and whether it can bear
reality with love. After Ivan's dreadful indictment of the creation and of the apparent moral economics of a world in which
the creator budgets for the torture of children in the name of a
general good, there is indeed nothing that can be said in
response at that level. Any defence would have to stay within the
same discourse of 'economics' and try to show what Alyosha
rightly refuses to argue, that the world is really worthwhile in
spite of the pain and abuse of the innocent.

   Dostoyevsky's reply moves in a quite different direction.
Say that Ivan is right; say that the world cannot be 'justified'
and its creator cannot be defended. We are still left with the
question of how we are to live in it, what we bring to it. We can
try to conceal the real nature of the world from others out of
the Inquisitor's poignant mixture of pity and the hunger for
power; we can elect to live meaninglessly, collaborating, so
to speak, with the intrinsic destructiveness of things
(like Golding's Sophy) or simply exploring our sensations
(like Ivan). The kiss that the prisoner gives to the Inquisitor is
another possibility, however – groundless, if you like, but
possible, and expressing a radical valuation of humanity,
dependent upon nothing but love, denying nothing. The
Inquisitor's perspective assumes one central truth: the basic

orientation of the world towards death and emptiness. His love for humanity is ultimately a desperate wish to protect it from reality. But what is such a perspective to make of someone who asks for no protection, yet does not react with either despair or violence?

The Inquisitor cannot cope. He wants an answer in *his* language, even if it is an annihilating sentence, but there is no answer except the affirmation that a kind of love is possible that is greater than his protective but oppressive pity. His world can only struggle to shut this out. If you grant that such a love is really possible, then the rationale of protecting humanity falls away. The tragedy of the Inquisitor is that he cannot bring himself, ultimately, to kill Jesus. He expels him, but still lets him live, and is haunted from then on by the kiss Jesus gave him. He acknowledges the truth of the perspective and response that his entire system is designed to ignore, but he cannot include the whole or the heart of human possibility. There is the logic of Alyosha's kiss for Ivan. It is a way of saying, with the Inquisitor's prisoner, that Ivan's story of the world leaves out something fundamental. The kiss no more establishes a defence for God the creator than Jesus' kiss explains why the Inquisitor is wrong. Say that God is indefensible, that the Inquisitor is right, and it is still possible to see reality with love, however tormented, however restless, angry or heartbroken.

The object of love

It has often been said that the God of *The Brothers Karamazov* is not the God of orthodoxy (or Orthodoxy in the narrower sense). It has also been said that there is no God at all 'behind' the figure of Jesus in Ivan's story. In an important sense, these observations are true – perhaps truer than Dostoyevsky himself knew – but they take us at once back to Robert Aske, hanging in chains at York, clinging to 'that holy, that merciful, which though not God, though vanquished, was still the last dear love of a vanquished and tortured man'.[10] The point of the fable of the Inquisitor is very much that of Mark's Gospel: God becomes recognizable as God only at the place of extremity, where no answers seem to be given and God cannot be seen as the God we expect or understand.

Yet, if God is somehow recognized in such a place, in the reality of a loving embrace of the tormented world, it still does not give us any theory about why the universe is as it is, or why human beings are capable of unspeakable cruelties towards the innocent. It simply tells us that humanity can be taken with the immense seriousness of unreserved love and asserts that this, not any other response, is the one perception which is adequate to the truth. In showing us a humanity groundlessly occasioning such love, it puts before us the vision of a humanity that is actually and timelessly the object of love. We could go further and say that only such a vision of humanity makes sense of the anguish and anger of Ivan's vision – for, if humanity is only the doomed and deluded herd of the Inquisitor's imagining, why is the death of a child so unforgivable an outrage?

10 Prescott, *The Man on a Donkey*, p. 765.

What happens to the judges?

Perhaps the Inquisitor cannot kill Jesus because he knows – so Ivan seems to suggest – that what is true in his own distorted compassion for humanity depends on his prisoner after all. To kill Jesus would be a self-mutilation that he cannot carry through. Once again, we are reminded that the Inquisitor is a deeply tragic figure, not a caricature of totalitarian villainy. But what of the judge who *did* kill the prisoner?

I mentioned earlier on the fantasies of some Christian writers about the punishments visited on the enemies of Jesus and his Church. There is a whole distressing cluster of medieval texts about this, called the *Avengings of the Saviour*, describing the terrible things that happened to Caiaphas, Pilate and Antipas.[11] The New Testament already opens the door to this with the lurid account of Judas' death in Acts 1. Nonetheless, buried in this uncomfortable literature is a question about the effect of Jesus' condemnation on his judges which cannot be brushed off simply as revenge fantasy. Ivan's Inquisitor seems to recognize that his condemnation of Jesus is a *self*-condemnation. One of the most evocative moments in the fable is the long silence in which he waits for the prisoner's reply. It is another Russian writer, however, who takes this up and explores it fully – the twentieth-century novelist Mikhail Bulgakov, in his masterpiece entitled *The Master and Margarita*.

It is impossible to summarize adequately this wildly satirical and surreal book. It is a portrait of Stalinist Moscow,

11 Examples can be found in M.R. James, *The Apocryphal New Testament*, corrected edition, Oxford: Clarendon Press, 1953, pp. 155ff.

interwoven with a fictional reconstruction of the passion story, partly narrated by the devil (who is visiting Moscow for a few weeks), and partly by the 'Master' of the title. The Master, a dissident novelist, has been silenced by the subtle threats and pressures of the regime, yet is unable to let go of the questions posed in his own secret fiction about Christ. The novel works at many levels, and the chapters on the passion story are not only an oblique reflection of Stalinist tyranny, complete with secret agents, quiet diplomatic murders and the ever-present memory of all-powerful Caesar, but also an agonized examination of literary cowardice and betrayal, the willingness under pressure to push the real life of the imagination out of sight. Bulgakov is commenting on his own struggles and failures as a nonconforming intellectual in Stalin's Russia as well as satirizing the massive public stupidity of the regime. So the Pilate of the story is the novelist as well as the novelist's enemies in the state bureaucracy, and the question raised in the fiction is whether, once truth has been denied, there is ever a second chance.

Pilate's unfinished conversation

The Pilate in this story is a tough and brutal character, intensely lonely, devoted only to his dog and suffering from appalling migraines. Jesus is a none too articulate holy simpleton who addresses everyone as 'good man', including the governor. In an unforgettably bold reversal of expectations, Bulgakov rewrites the dialogue about truth from John's Gospel:

'Why did you stir up the people in the bazaar, you vagrant, talking about the truth, of which you have no notion? What is truth?'

And here the procurator thought: 'Oh, my gods! I'm asking him about something unnecessary at a trial . . . my reason no longer serves me . . .' And again he pictured a cup of dark liquid. 'Poison, bring me poison . . .'

And again he heard the voice: 'The truth is, first of all, that your head aches, and aches so badly that you're having faint-hearted thoughts of death . . . And I am now your unwilling torturer, which upsets me. You can't even think about anything and only dream that your dog should come, apparently the only being you are attached to.'[12]

This is anything but a frivolous version of events. The truth really is that Pilate is suffering, and it is at this moment the truth that matters for the dishevelled young philosopher who stands before the governor. The truth is indeed that Pilate is both tormented and comforted by Yeshua, his prisoner. When he is finally manipulated by the High Priest into signing the death warrant, he knows that something of enormous moment has occurred. Later that day, he tries to deny to himself the anguish he feels. 'It was clear to him that that afternoon he had lost something irretrievably, and that he now wanted to make up for the loss by some petty, worthless and, above all, belated actions'.[13] He has just arranged the

12 Mikhail Bulgakov, *The Master and Margarita*, trans. Richard Pevear and Larissa Volokhonsky, London: Penguin, 1997, p. 24.
13 Ibid., p. 310.

assassination of Judas Iscariot as a small gesture of revenge for what he has been forced to do.

What becomes of Pilate? Bulgakov picks up the medieval legend that he haunts one of the Alpine peaks and gives it a poignant new turn. Pilate sits for ever on his mountain top, alone with his dog, sleeping, except when the moon is full (as it was at the Passover). 'Margarita saw that the seated man, whose eyes seemed blind, rubbed his hands fitfully, and peered with those same unseeing eyes at the disc of the moon.' He talks to himself, saying always:

> ... one and the same thing ... that even the moon gives him no peace, and that his is a bad job. That is always what he says when he is not asleep, and when he sleeps, he dreams one and the same thing: there is a patch of moonlight, and he wants to walk down it and talk with the prisoner Ha-Nozri, because, as he insists, he never finished what he was saying that time, long ago, on the fourteenth day of the spring month of Nisan.[14]

The conversation with Yeshua is not only the great lost opportunity of Pilate's life. The fact that it was begun and interrupted has left him, it seems, eternally suspended between worlds, frozen in a moment of pain and confusion. For his history to go on, he must be able once again to speak with the 'philosopher', even though he has no idea what could possibly be said. Mysteriously, however, there is hope for him.

14 Ibid., p. 381.

Margarita, the novelist's mistress, who has bargained and pleaded with the devil for more than one desperate soul during her bizarre encounters with the supernatural forces at work in the action of the novel, now begs for Pilate's release – only to receive from Satan the answer, 'You don't need to ask for him, Margarita, because the one he so yearns to talk with has already asked for him.'[15]

The Master, says Satan, can now finish his novel at a stroke, and the novelist cries to Pilate, 'You're free! You're free! He's waiting for you!' A moonlit path opens up, and dog and man run down it to start once again the all-important conversation which had been interrupted by the moment of judgement and betrayal. 'The man in the white cloak with blood-red lining rose from the armchair and shouted something in a hoarse, cracked voice. It was impossible to tell whether he was weeping or laughing, or what he shouted. It could only be seen that, following his faithful guardian, he, too, rushed headlong down the path of moonlight.'[16]

Peace and light

His fate is deliberately set alongside that of the Master and Margarita. The Master, we have been told earlier, has been granted 'peace', but not 'light'. It is Pilate who is given leave to go into the light of Yeshua's presence, into the active, perhaps purgatorial, but surely indispensable exchange of conversation with truth. The Master and the woman who loves him are settled in an 'eternal home', still and gentle, surrounded by

15 Ibid., p. 382.
16 Ibid., pp. 382–3.

cherry trees, where at night they can listen to Schubert by candlelight.[17] It is a liberation of a kind for the tormented novelist, but Bulgakov – who entitles this chapter 'Forgiveness and Eternal Refuge' – is clearly drawing a distinction between the liberation of some kind of re-creation through an encounter with Yeshua and the liberation of sheer security, an eternalizing of what makes us feel most deeply at home.

Pilate's destiny is open in a way the Master's is not. The power that allots these destinies recognizes the ache and hunger in Pilate and also recognizes that the Master has in some way refused something crucial. It is related to the theme that keeps recurring in the novel: the real nature of cowardice. It is, finally, treated with the greatest compassion, but it is obviously a barrier to reaching both the light and transformation. As for Margarita, she chooses her love for the Master as her final and greatest good – her future will be to 'watch over' the Master as he sleeps, to be with him as his memory gradually melts away into the eternal present of 'peace'. There is no hint of condemnation, but the bare fact that this is not actually the *truth* is not softened for us in any way.

What Bulgakov is doing is reflecting on the choices made by people under duress, especially when faced with the pressure to decide for or against what they know is truth, when nothing is humanly to be gained by opting for truth. The cowardice of turning away, denying what has been authoritatively seen (the Master has burned his novel about Pilate, just as Bulgakov himself burned an early draft of *his* novel and concealed the text for decades), means not damnation in a conventional sense, but simple diminution, a world in which

17 Ibid., pp. 384–5.

no saving change can occur, in which we have already made our bargain with life.

Risking the truth

When we were looking at John's Gospel, we saw that the questions posed for us in Jesus' trial all had to do with one simple issue – whether or not we wanted to be where Jesus is. Our failures are all about our fearful longing to be somewhere else. Bulgakov shows us the cost: peace before light; a sense of rest and absolution without the reality of re-creation. The Master is given a compassionate discharge, we might say, left exhausted with the consolations of art and human love. There is no suggestion that these are evils or trivial things in themselves, but used as a defence against a truth that makes harsher demands, they acquire a kind of moral and spiritual shadow. They pose the same problems as the Inquisitor's compassion for humanity – they presume that there is less to human beings than in fact there is, even though that full human perspective involves such enormous risks.

Perhaps, then, what is on trial in the trial of Jesus could also be described as the whole complex of human consolations. Under the spotlight in Mark are the consolations of religion: the confidence that God will finally yield to our theories and our expectations, the assurance that God's transcendence in fact leaves relatively untouched the ways in which human beings set their priorities and understand their hopes or desires. Matthew elaborates on this: instead of the shock of divine Wisdom in its actuality, we are consoled by our own wisdom, by our sense of expertise in the business of religious behaviour and religious talk, increasingly independent of

God. For Luke, the consolation under scrutiny is that of knowing oneself to be an 'insider', not having to listen to the voices of strangers, confident about whose voice counts and whose does not. John glosses this further by setting the world God loves, the world we are called to be at home in and with, against the world tidied and organized by our wills and imaginations. The consolation he pinpoints is that of not being where we are, inhabiting instead the world of which we are in charge.

Looking at the history of the martyrs, flawed and ambiguous as it often is, we can see that the inducements to accept a shrunken and inadequate world are enormous, and the costs of refusing it are correspondingly enormous and painful. Our concluding look at how the fate of Jesus' judges might be imagined simply asks whether the cost of refusing the full scale of our own humanity can genuinely be thought of as outweighing the cost of the pain caused by embracing a reality we do not control.

The test of the cross

There is a Latin expression associated with late medieval and Reformation religious thought which sums up much of what these chapters have been about: *experimentum crucis* – literally 'the experience of the cross', but also, by an obvious extension of meaning, the test, the 'experiment' of the cross, the way in which, in our own self-understanding, the cross tries and probes us. One of the rather depressing things about a good deal of theology concerning the cross of Jesus is that it can give the impression (unintentionally, of course) of directing our attention purely and simply to what is done for us by Jesus' crucifixion, thus directing our attention away from the question of exactly how that crucifixion is rooted in who and what we are.

To speak of it only as an 'external' settling of debts will not do. While it is essential to see the passion of Jesus as something that freely works, independently of our effort, to renew and heal us, that very healing and renewal come to their fullness only as we absorb in heart and mind what it is in us that calls out for healing. Hence the significance of reflecting on the history of the passion, and in particular on the stories of the trial. As we have seen time and time again in these pages, the question we are left with as we read is about who *we* are. The various ways in which we can ask Jesus who *he* is, summed up in the variety of ways he is cross-examined by his judges, tell us where we are coming from, what it is in us that is afraid of the prisoner in the dock.

Once we have started to see how these fears work, we are better placed to see also how they are activated in our world, in our relationships. Part of the purpose of this book has been to suggest how the trial of Jesus is re-enacted in our contemporary experience; how the *experimentum crucis* comes to us in the shape of the small and large crises of encounters with strangers and outsiders now; how it comes alive in the Church's constant struggle not to become the object of its own faith; how it is as possible as ever today to betray for the sake of what we think is peace.

Making sense of the resurrection

You might think that there has been very little about resurrection in this book, and in one sense you would be right. It might seem as though the essential message has been that truth makes demands upon us that have to be met without hope of reward or reparation, that the cost of integrity is, ultimately, the death of human aspiration. This would leave us, surely, with a Stoic heroism rather than a Christian holiness. Here I think the Christian faces a particularly tough dilemma, for the more we *talk* about resurrection and healing, the more we risk slipping into another version of the world's morality – pain now, perhaps, but plenty of things to make up for it later on. Yet the refusal to talk of resurrection is at least as much of a problem. Christianity has never spoken of the cross as an isolated thing: the cross tells us who it is who is proclaimed as risen and triumphant – and that implies that the praises of the Risen One are the first words of the infant Church.

Perhaps what we find difficult is that we have largely lost any vivid sense of how the resurrection set a new agenda for the infant Church. Judging from the Gospel accounts, far from being first and foremost a simple fulfilling of expectations, a confirmation of what had already been said and believed, the resurrection seems to have been mysterious, baffling, something that threw expectations off balance and which carried its own sense of a call to trial and judgement. It was understood as a gift coming out of real and definitive darkness, loss and death, not a happy ending or a reversal of tragedy. If it is to be that for us too, we have to live *through* the process, not just rush straight on to the conclusion. Faith in the resurrection is necessarily related to the *experimentum crucis*, the 'cross-examination' in which our untruths are laid bare to us and we lose the consolations of having a clear image of ourselves and how we stand before God.

As the confidence we may have in our wisdom and integrity drains away, confronted with the prisoner in the dock, and as we realize the many ways in which it is still possible to betray and judge him in our fear and evasiveness, so much more does the 'density' of reality gather around the prisoner. If we come to the point of recognizing in him the absolute priority and otherness of God, it is at the price of having everything we are most sure of about ourselves and our resources brought into question. Yet it is at just this moment that we are at last free to see in Jesus the act that cannot be exhausted or confined, the act of the creator. The events that open out to us what I have earlier called a 'hospitable' truth, the possibility of being at home in the world, are not simply a moment in the world's history, but a point at which the welcoming reality of God breaks through the network of human transactions.

At precisely this point we can begin to make sense of the resurrection. Violence and death cannot end or extinguish the act that is present in Jesus. His condemnation and execution are not a terrible story of human iniquity and heroic resistance, but a glimpse of God – a glimpse of God in the utter difference from us and our expectations that so strains our language to breaking point. When the first believers proclaim that Jesus is alive and has met with them in recognizable (though strange) form, they are thus filling out the logic of what has been seen in the trial. The act of God that judges us remains active as it always was. God has been active in Jesus, including the suffering and rejected Jesus, and God will never cease to be active in him.

Historically, all this must have been a densely confused and confusing process – the experience of encounter with the risen Jesus prompting constant reworking and retelling of the trial and passion stories; the passion stories checking any tendency for the resurrection narratives to become triumphalist vindications of the Church's faith, devoid of their own edge of challenge and disturbance. We modern readers, however, inevitably begin from the resurrection faith witnessed in our own baptism and Christian practice. Our danger, therefore, is that we risk taking the resurrection for granted. We shall only experience the resurrection in its true *strangeness* if we can work back to the judgement of Jesus on trial. When we have faced that question and pondered its implications, we may be more ready to see how the resurrection creates its own new agenda – more ready to see, in fact, why there is a New Testament at all, let alone a Church or a creed.

The unavoidable encounter

The Christian gospel tells us not simply that we are saved from sin or that our guilt is taken away – it insists that we shall find out who we are and what we may be in an encounter, a relationship. All human identity is constructed through conversations, in one way and another. The gospel adds the news that, in order to find the pivot of our identity as human beings, there is one inescapable encounter, one all-important conversation into which we must be drawn. This is not just the encounter with God, in a general sense, but the encounter with God made vulnerable, God confronting the systems and exclusions of the human world *within* that world – so that, among other things, we can connect the encounter with God to those human encounters where we are challenged to listen to the outsider and the victim.

The Gospels, the history of the Church, the imaginative constructions of novelists like Dostoyevsky and Bulgakov, all

give us a picture of the variety of stratagems we use to avoid
that conversation, and of the cost of such avoidance. Whatever
pushes us to the limits of understanding and makes us
strangers to ourselves is capable of challenging or halting our
longing for avoidance. This does not mean that we seek out
extreme situations so as to test ourselves. The whole point is
that we do not arrange our own testing, because that not only
stays within the realm of our familiar world but also feeds our
sense of the dramatic, which is perhaps the one thing most
inimical to the kind of truthfulness demanded by the 'experiment of the cross'.

While we cannot arrange what trials we shall have to face,
however, we can in some ways prepare, if only by developing
the habit of putting ourselves before Jesus as he stands in the
court, putting ourselves under scrutiny and learning to question our behaviour and definitions, our image of ourselves
and the human world. One thing that is central to our
encounter with Jesus on trial is our willingness to be silent, to
let *his* silence work upon us, and to sense his gaze upon us.
Luke has left us one searing image of this, when he concludes
his account of Peter's betrayal with the words, 'The Lord
turned and looked straight at Peter, and Peter remembered'
(Luke 22:61).

He may have meant that Jesus literally passed through the
courtyard at that moment; he may have been guessing what
the effect of the cock crowing must have been on Peter – as if
Jesus' scrutiny was turned directly on him as his memory was
awakened. It does not greatly matter. All the stories and all our
reflections on them come back to the vital awareness that
here, in Jesus' presence, we are seen before we ourselves
see. We had thought *we* were the ones doing things, asking,

looking, probing. Suddenly it is someone else who is acting and we realize that we are the ones acted on, looked at, tried. The trial of Jesus, as I have said often enough, is about establishing his identity, not about gathering details on what he has done. As soon as we begin to see what the answer to that question of identity is, we see ourselves, our own identities, coming to light under his eyes. The Old Testament asks whether a human being can see God and live. These stories pose for us another question: whether we can *be seen* by God and live.

We cannot. Or rather, the 'we' or the 'I' with whom we are satisfied cannot be seen by God and live. At the end of the trial, we must yield ourselves up to the truth, put ourselves in the hands of the only power that can give life. This requires a trust we are not used to, a trust that comes into being only when we know and accept that we are loved. Our response is longed for by the living truth. 'You're free! He's waiting for you!'

Questions for reflection and discussion

1 Have you ever, like Job, wanted to put God on trial for the sufferings of the world?

2 How much difference do you believe it can make to a suffering person to know that he or she is loved?

3 Which word best expresses what you long for in God's presence – 'peace' or 'light'?

4 Is the resurrection of Jesus simply a 'happy ending', or is it something more?

5 Have you felt in the life or presence of someone
around you the presence of Jesus, judging you or
comforting you, or both?

Prayer

Jesus,
give us the courage to let ourselves be judged by you,
and the courage to let ourselves be loved by you;
and as you come to us, risen from the dead,
help us to hear and respond when you say,
'Don't be afraid.'
Amen.